THE BEAR PROJECT

How a Jack Russell named Bear grew her Angel Wings

JODY CROSSLEY

First published in Australia 2022 by Jody Crossley

ISBN 978-0-6456213-0-3

Disclaimer

All the information, techniques, skills and concepts contained within this publication are of the nature of general comment only, and are not in any way recommended as individual advice. The intent is to offer a variety of information to provide a wider range of choices now and in the future, recognising that we all have widely diverse circumstances and viewpoints. Should any reader choose to make use of the information herein, this is their decision, and the author and publisher/s do not assume any responsibilities whatsoever under any conditions or circumstances. The author does not take responsibility for the business, financial, personal or other success, results or fulfilment upon the readers' decision to use this information. It is recommended that the reader obtain their own independent advice.

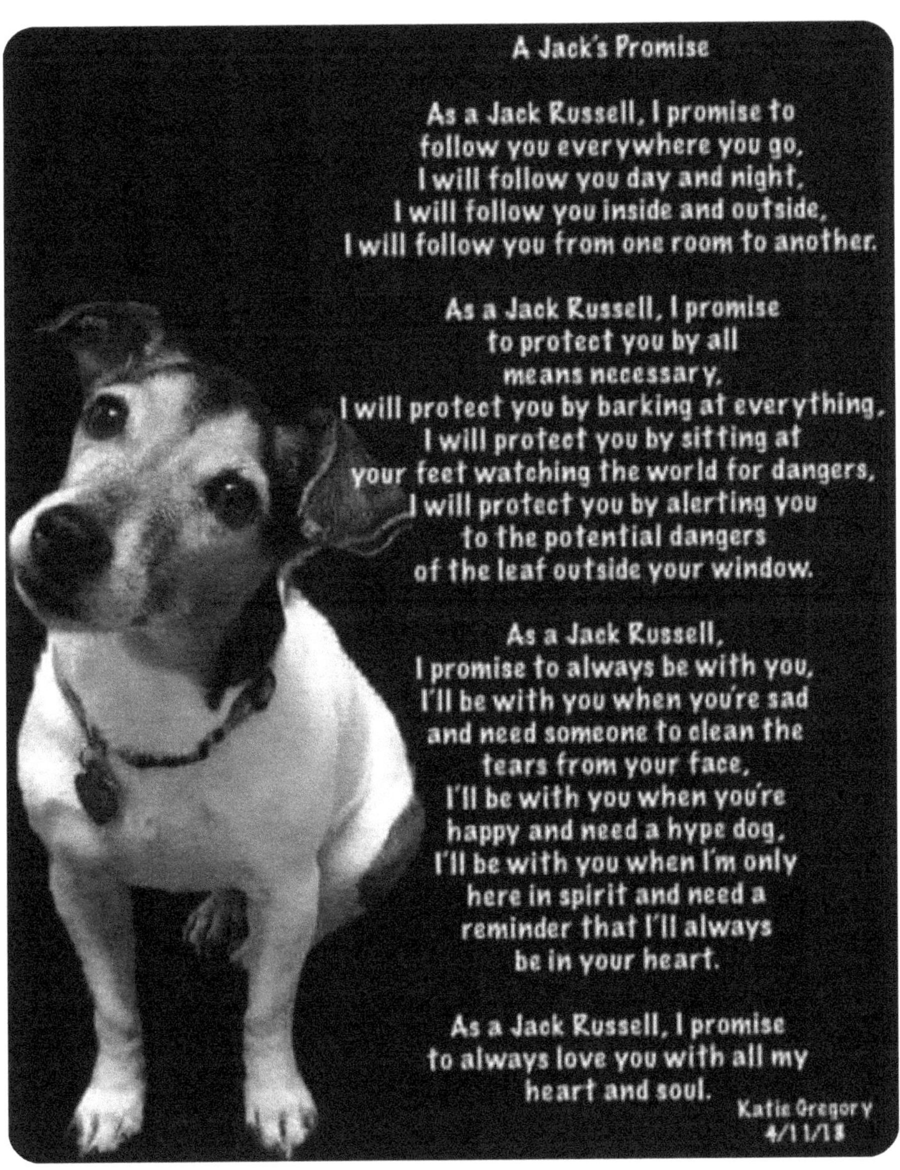

Credit Katie Gregory - A Jacks Promise : jackrussellterrier (reddit.com)

A very big thank you to my sponsors.
This book could not have been published without you.

Physioinq South Penrith / Penrith
Owner & Principal Physiotherapist: Christopher Slaviero
https://www.southpenrithphysio.com.au

Kelly's Animal Communication
Owner: Kelly Mercieca
www.kellysanimalcommunication.com.au

JB Fabweld
Jason Bradshaw
jbbfabweld@gmail.com

Pet Bereavement Counsellor
Sharlene Crofts
sharlenescounsellingservices@yahoo.com

Bovercon Pty Ltd
Director: Edward Breedveld
www.bovercon.com.au

Comfort Cuddles
Kaylene Dore
www.comfortcuddles.com.au

Assistance Dogs in Training Australia
Kaylene Dore
https://www.adita.com.au/

Rotary Club of Wallacia
Mulgoa Valley
https://www.facebook.com/pages/category/Nonprofit-organization/Rotary-Club-of-Wallacia-Mulgoa-Valley-Australia-114479565269822/

Penrith Veterinary Hospital
www.penrithvet.com.au

Kristine's K9 Treats
https://www.kristinesk9kakesandtreats.com.au

Selwood House Vet Hospital
Selwood House Vet Hospital (selwoodvets.com.au)

By My Side Pet Bereavement Counselling
Vicky Nonas
www.bymyside.net.au

Dedication

First and foremost, the biggest dedication goes to my beloved best friend Bear (1/6/2005-16/11/2021). My soulmate, my heart, my partner in crime. There will never be another you. You are irreplaceable; I will love you forever. Until we meet again, RIP sweet Bear. Mum will see you again one day.

This book is dedicated to all those who are experiencing the loss and grief of their beloved pet. Remember that pets are not just dogs, cats and horses, but can be ferrets, birds and other animals, too. Don't let anyone ever say your pet is just an animal. Only people like you and me understand the true meaning of a bond with a pet. Our pets are like children who reach out to us on levels where some humans are unable to reach us.

I have a favourite term which I use a lot: animals won't hurt you, but people will hurt you and let you down. Show an animal kindness, and they will give you their heart and soul.

Poem by Ed Breedveld (sponsor)

The Day You Left by Ed Breedveld

That fateful day is burned in my mind, and one that I'll forever feel
Your memory will always be playing like photos spinning on a reel
I stare into rooms nowadays empty and sad
Remembering so many good times we had
From times holding you in my hand when you were so small
To times in the yard playing with a rope or a ball
Times when I was down, feeling ill, sad, or blue
These were the times I could always rely on you
Though you could not speak, you still offered love at no cost
To heal me and guide me when I was feeling lost
Part of me died with you on the day that you went
Heaven had surely regained the angel that it sent
So, thank you for sharing your time with me and being the sun that brightened my night
For the flame of love that you ignited within me, will forever burn bright.

♥

Reasons for writing this book

There are five main reasons why I wrote this book. I was once asked, why write a book? You are not a writer, so why now? The answer is, no, I am not a writer. I have never done anything like this in my life, and to be honest, part of me is terrified. Here are the reasons I wrote it:

1. First, to help me process my grief. Two very wise and wonderful ladies, Dina Franks and Alison Tadic, told me to write a letter and put my feelings out there. I went one step further and wrote a book. Who would have thought?

2. To honour my best friend, Bear. She was my inspiration. She gave me courage, love, laughter, sheer happiness, loyalty, commitment, undivided attention, and never judged me. She accepted me just as I was. But, most of all, she gave me a purpose, and even though she has crossed over to the Rainbow Bridge, she provided me with an even bigger purpose – to share what I've learned.

3. To help others process their grief and let them know they are not alone, even though this journey may feel lonely, with no light at the end of the tunnel. I have found solace and comfort in the company of complete strangers. There is always someone who will show you kindness and compassion and listen and lend a shoulder.

4. To shine a light on our vet professionals. Depression is common within the veterinary industry, and suicide rates high. Vet Life Australia (the website of Australian Veterinary Mental Health Awareness and Suicide prevention) reports the following: 30.6% of veterinarians suffer stress and 25.6% of veterinarians suffer from depression. These professionals do amazing things

with patients who can't describe the depth of their pain or where it hurts. Our pets rely on us to provide their medical history and behaviours to our vets so they can start running the appropriate tests. I want people to realise how hard a job vets have – not only the pressures they face, but the ugly side of pet ownership they face, such as abused and abandoned animals. I also want to highlight the practise of euthanasia. This affects vets too, especially when they bond with pets and their owners. Vets are the forgotten ones in this journey.

5. To highlight the need for greater respect for pet owners in the workplace. I think it is about time we were treated equally and fairly as pet parents, just like everyone else. Pet parents are treated far differently from those parents with children. I want workplaces to discourage their employees from expressing the sentiment that it was just a pet, and can therefore easily be replaced. People who express this view are the ones I feel truly sorry for. They have missed out on an incredible journey that a pet can take us on; our fur babies are better than half the population out there in this crazy world. Grief is very real, and workplaces, more than ever, need to better support grieving pet parents.

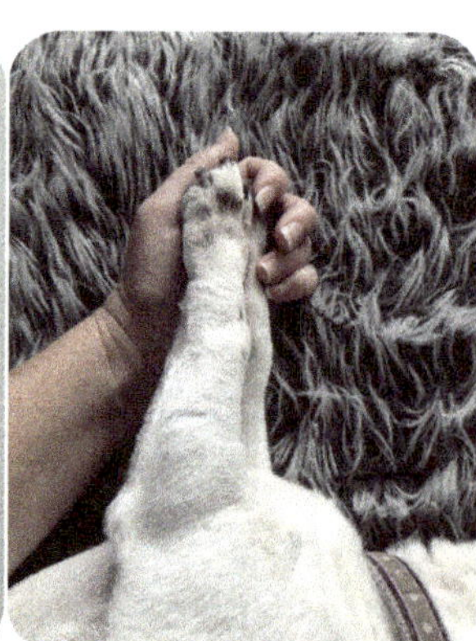

Table of Contents

PART 1

The Journey

Grief

I started writing this book in the early stages of grief. Bear grew her angel wings on Tuesday 16th November 2021 at 6:30 p.m. I started writing this book on Friday 26th November 2021.

I would like to start by saying I have no medical background, knowledge or experience. Nor have I studied any form of degree within a medical field. These are my own thoughts, experiences and feelings. It is my personal journey of grief. I hope by sharing my experience I am able to help comfort and reassure others so they can get through this. I am living proof.

People mean well and sometimes don't know the right things to say. The things people said which tended to make me angry were "It will just take time," and my favourite, "This is the new normal" or "How are you?" It is hard to find the words to reach out to someone when they are grieving. Unfortunately, there are no words and no magic pill or medication. It is funny, in a world full of medical advancements, we still can't mend a broken heart from grief. They say chest pain, even after tests on your heart come back fine, is where the term "broken heart" comes from. I believe this. I have a broken heart.

Up until losing Bear, I had never really experienced chest pain or even panic attacks – however I now know what it is like to experience both. The grieving process can not only affect us mentally and emotionally, but physically as well. I know since losing Bear my Crohn's Disease has flared up, and I am stressed. As hard as grieving is, we really need to make sure we take care of ourselves. In a lot of cases there are others who need us – children, family members and other pets.

What is grief?

Grief is an emotion that really can't be understood if you haven't experienced it. It is an emotion only those who have lived through can genuinely feel and describe. People have said that grieving for a person and a pet are different. I know a few people who have said they have lost a person and a pet and believe losing a pet is definitely harder. I can't touch on this subject as I haven't lost a person close to me yet. I like to describe grief and break it down as below:

G – Gut-wrenching – there are no words. You feel like you are broken, like a piece of you has died, that you are shattered and can't breathe. You feel like the wind has been knocked out of you, like you can't move forward, or you don't want to. How does life go on from here without your best friend by your side?

R – Relentless – the pain feels like it is never-ending. It is a numbing sensation. You almost feel like you're in a nightmare which you can't wake up from. You wake up and go to sleep with it (if you can sleep), and it is there twenty-four hours a day.

I – Inconsolable – It doesn't matter what anyone says or does, who you speak to on the phone or how many hugs you receive or even how much crying you do, the pain is still there, and you can't see how it will get better. You can't imagine moving forward without your beloved pet by your side. You look around the house and there are constant reminders everywhere you turn.

E – Exhausting – You can't sleep, you can't eat (loss of appetite), you are mentally and emotionally exhausted, you are running on empty.

I felt like I was in a body going through the motions but not really there and not really wanting to be present in the moment. I felt like I was drowning and no one could hear me.

F – Fractured – You feel like you are lost, like you will never be whole again. A big part of you is gone. Heartbroken and shattered, you feel like a piece of you has died and gone to heaven with your pet.

When you look up the word "grief" in the dictionary, you get this description:

Grief - definition of grief by The Free Dictionary

Grief (gri:f) n 1. **deep or intense sorrow or distress,** especially at the death of someone 2. something that causes keen distress or suffering 3. informal trouble or annoyance: "people were giving me grief for leaving ten minutes early."

You honestly feel like you're dying a slow, painful death and there is nothing you can do. I had a wise friend tell me it is the small milestones (goals) you achieve through each day, like sitting in the sun, having a cry when you need to, and not forgetting the simple things like making your bed, having a shower, combing your hair and brushing your teeth. These small milestones will help you get through each day.

I took time off work for five days. I needed to do this, but it wasn't good for my grief. I had no structure, so I sat around and cried and cried and cried some more, to the point I could barely see out of my eyes. I found by going back to work I had no choice but to focus on something other than the loss of Bear and my grief. Bills and rent still needed to be paid. My grief would still be there when I finished work.

When I returned to work, I drew up a daily to-do list. I started with the simplest things, and then, as each week passed, I would add another one or two things to the list, as you can see in the example below. This is not set in concrete. Set your own small goals, based on what you feel you can achieve. It is normal if one day you simply find you are unable to accomplish the tasks.

There were a few days when I just couldn't get dressed or do my hair or makeup, and that's okay. The grieving process has stages, and you go at your own pace. Remember, there is no time limit. Grief comes in waves. One day you feel like you are semi-coping and the next day you will be in absolute pieces and shattered. There are no rights and wrongs to grieving. Everyone grieves differently in their own way.

TO-DO LIST Week 1	TO-DO LIST Week 2
• Make my bed	• WORK
• Get dressed	• Make my bed
• Do my hair	• Get dressed
• Put on some makeup	• Do my hair
• EAT	• Put on some make up

We can't let grief win. We can't let it drag us into that deep, dark hole called depression. Depression can be very hard to overcome. I have been there, and I almost took my own life (I will touch on this later in the book).

That is not what our pets would want for us. They would want for us to continue on our path. After all, they were sent to us for a purpose. What that purpose was, only you will know. I know what Bear's purpose was for me, and I will explain later in the book. I am not an overly religious person, but I do believe there is a God and I do believe our pets go to heaven or the Rainbow Bridge. I look back at the precious bond and memories I formed with Bear and I know deep down in my heart she would want me to be happy, to continue on with my life and remember with fondness all the memories we created and shared.

She would also be telling me from up above in her sassy, bossy way, "Mum, you have four other fur babies – my siblings who need you." Bear would also be telling me, "I made you whole again and I didn't come to you in the first place for you to give up now." I believe Bear has grown angel wings and is doing work for God now. She did what she was meant to on earth when God sent her to me – and that was to heal me. She would not want me to give up now, just as your pets wouldn't want you to give up on life.

I also believe that when the time is right and we have done our grieving, our pets will act in a way of divine intervention. What does this mean, you ask? This means they know how much love each one of us has to give, and I believe when the time is right, they will send the next Earth angel to love. We need to remember, just because we can no longer touch them or see them doesn't mean they don't see us and are not watching our every move (in-between playing with other dogs and balls). But first, we must let go of them, grieve, never forget, always cherish their memories, but reopen our heart. Let's face it, there are so many abandoned, abused animals in shelters who need a human of their own who will love them and protect them.

I know that Bear would want another pet to experience the amazing life she had with her siblings and me. There is no time limit on when you should or shouldn't get another pet. Just remember you're not getting another pet to replace them: they are irreplaceable. Sometimes, people need that new pet to help them with their grief, help them love again and give them a reason to keep moving forward.

There is no right or wrong way to do this. You do what you feel is right for you and what will help you deal with the grief. Everyone will go on their own journey of grief, and you do what you feel is right for you. No one else's opinions matter. People can comment that it isn't the right time, or it is too soon, but they are not walking the path of grief. Please remember, if the grief is too overwhelming, reach out to a professional for help.

The only rule I have with grief is that you don't give up, and that you keep taking small, slow steps each day. It is okay not to want to celebrate events, but don't shut people out from your life. The greatest gift people gave me was their time, love and support, and this did help me with my grief. The other thing was talking about Bear. I am still not at a point where I can talk about her and not cry and sob, but I know the day will come when I can talk about all the happy times, have a laugh about the funny things she did and shed a tear, but it won't be so painful.

In the chapter *My journey*, I will describe how she saved me, and her reason for coming into my life. As much as you may want to give up, there are reasons we need to continue – our loved ones, children and other fur babies. Remember, the pain is very real right now. It will get easier over time, but if we give up, we cause pain for the others we leave behind.

Overcoming grief does take time. No two people are going to grieve the same way or for the same amount of time. There is no time limit. Don't let anyone tell you, "You should be over it by now" or "You need to just move on and think of the happy times." Take the time you need and do what you need to move forward.

I find that grief comes in waves. One minute I can feel okay, and then I can cry for the next few hours and not stop. Some days seem to be harder for some reason. I haven't worked out why this is. Sometimes there can be triggers like a song or an advertisement or a favourite toy. I found myself waking up some days and knew from the moment I opened my eyes this was going to be one of those particularly hard days.

I don't honestly feel I will ever be whole again. Bear took a piece of me with her when she left for the Rainbow Bridge. I know that hole will never heal, but the love for her and the bond we shared will keep me going for the rest of my life.

People told me Bear would tell me when it was her time, or I would just know. I kept asking how. I truly didn't understand this statement. I will discuss how Bear told me it was her time in the chapter about her last few days. I now know what people meant by this.

Bear had been sick on and off for a few years, but she was a true fighter and overcame every hurdle. As much as I would like to think that especially in the last six months of my life, I was realising each day was a milestone and precious and I didn't truly know if she would be alive much longer, I was certainly not prepared for this thing called grief. I am a strong person who has overcome a lot in life.

Most things I have been through some people have never been through in an entire lifetime. Losing Bear was the hardest thing I have gone through. If there is one thing you take away from reading this book, it is that you don't let grief WIN and, more importantly, be kind to yourself. Lean on others for support, especially on the bad days, but remember to hit those small milestones. The small milestones will eventually lead to bigger milestones.

Every morning, the first thing I would try to do was get dressed. It didn't always happen. Sometimes, I could barely function, let alone get dressed. At times, I felt like I was waking up to try and get dressed (put my armour on) to go into battle with my feelings and emotions.

I felt like I was at war, and it was not a war I felt I could win. I know almost every person out there experiencing grief will be feeling the exact same way.

I went to the supermarket the other day. I needed a smaller trolley as I only needed a few things. I got to the dog food section and looked at the Kangaroo, Super Coat biscuits Bear loved, and that triggered me. I left the supermarket in tears and raced out. People watched, probably thinking I was some crazy person. When I say there will be reminders and triggers everywhere, that is an understatement. It could be seeing someone walk a similar dog, a song, a pet store. (I cry almost every time I go past a pet store.)

I don't believe we ever get over the loss of our precious fur babies. I believe we just get better at coping with the fact they are gone. I know I will continue to have those days where I just cry, for many years to come. When I picked up Bear's urn the week after her passing, it felt like the grief had begun all over again. I will touch on this more in the chapter *Bear's last days.*

Writing this book about Bear has helped me with my grief. I feel like I am processing the grief and working through it. I also feel that not having it bottled up inside is helping me a great deal. Even if you sit and write a letter telling your pet how much you love them, how you are feeling, what they did to make you laugh and how they made you feel, it will help the grief. Once you start writing, you won't be able to stop, and by writing a little each day only when you feel up to it, you will process your thoughts and feelings. You can choose to share it with someone close to you or keep it just for yourself.

I am a member of a couple of pet loss groups on Facebook. There are so many people in these groups who are distraught, distressed, broken-hearted. Even grown men struggle to come to terms with the loss of their fur babies. There are people all over the world in the same position; we are not alone in this journey. It really helps to speak with people who know exactly how bad you are feeling.

There are so many sad stories about pets with cancer, pets that have been run over, pets that have had strokes or heart attacks, pets who've died at a young age and pets who lived right up to twenty-two years old. You're not the only one experiencing the loss of a pet, but in your moment of grief, you can feel like the only one living through grief, and it can feel very lonely. Some stories are even more heart-breaking, as some people have lost two pets in one month, from fretting or freak accidents. I remember reading one story where two dogs escaped through the owner's front door and were both hit by the same car. They both died whilst the owner watched helplessly.

I suggest joining a grief and loss group on Facebook. There are many, both local and overseas. It really does help to connect with others who are experiencing the same thoughts and feelings – like-minded people and people helping each other through a debilitating journey.

Remember: it's okay to not be okay. It is going to take time, so be kind and patient with yourself.

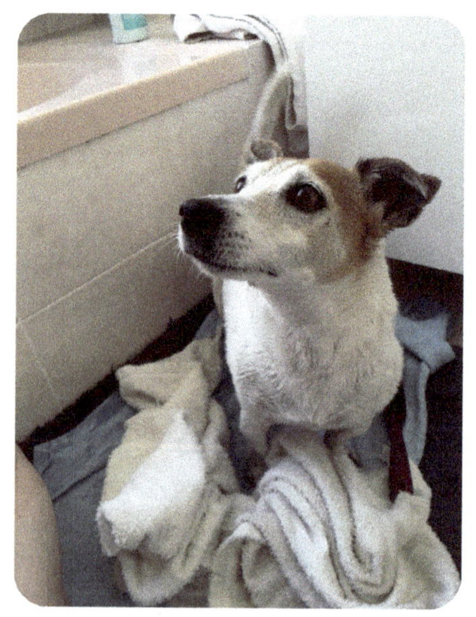

When we are grieving and going through the motions of grief, we need to ask ourselves constantly, "What would my pet want me to do? How would they want me to continue and move forward without them?" I think the simple answer to this question is to look for a purpose. It could be anything, such as writing a letter, volunteering at a local shelter, organising a fundraiser – this doesn't have to be pet-related. It could be something as simple as going to the gym, taking up a hobby or doing a course, or looking at changing a career path. You just need to have a reason to get out of the house and be around others to help form a new routine.

We all need a purpose, especially when dealing with grief. Your purpose is something only you will know, but it must be something that gets you out of bed to face the day – show up, so to speak. I know people firsthand who lost the only pet they had and ended up getting a new pet. By doing this, they weren't replacing the previous pet, but this new pet provided them with a purpose. I know of others who took up hobbies they had wanted to do for quite a while. One lady told me she took up pottery lessons, as she could zone out and concentrate on something other than grief. This also got her out of the house.

Only you will know what your purpose is. For me, it is writing this book to continue Bear's legacy, but to also help others. Having this purpose has helped me face the tough days and process my grief. I also went back to the gym, which helped me mentally process the grief and helped release good endorphins. I train with two other people who I had trained with previously, and found I began to enjoy this and formed a new routine.

I train around four times a week and find this really helps clear my mind (not forget about Bear) and gives me something other to focus on (my own mental health and well-being). When going through this rollercoaster ride called grief, you need a PURPOSE. Having a purpose is going to help you work through grief and also help you process your feelings and emotions. We still need to take care of ourselves and our health.

I look at grief as a worldwide pandemic. There are hundreds of thousands of people all over the world suffering with grief and the impact that losing a pet has on their life personally and professionally. This not only affects people in Australia, but all over the world. I think this is now the time to start bringing about awareness. It is needed now more than ever.

One thing I learnt about grief is that it does not discriminate, it does not care whether you are rich or poor, famous or homeless, young or old. It hits everyone with the same emotions and intensity. What is different about grief is that people will grieve for different lengths of time and in different ways.

Guilt

I feel guilt is such a big part of grief. I also believe guilt can hold you back from moving forward in the grieving process. Guilt consists of feelings and thoughts like "Did I wait too long to make the decision to say goodbye?" "Did I not wait long enough? Did I make a decision in haste?" The other components of guilt are the what if's: "What if I'd got a second opinion?" "What if I did the surgery?" "What if I'd changed medications and given her more time to fight this?" What ifs and guilt are not going to change the situation or the reality that sooner or later we will have to make that heart-breaking decision to say our goodbyes.

We really need to remember that our fur babies are a precious gift from God and were sent to us for a reason. The kindest thing we can do for them is end their pain and suffering. At the time, we feel we are not making the right decision by them to end their life, when in fact we are making the right one. In time, we will be able to look back and realise it was kinder to let them go and end the pain and suffering than to hold on to them because we can't say goodbye or bear to live without them.

Our pets would not want us to dwell or feel blame or guilt. After all, they knew how much we loved them and how much they loved us. They gave us the best of themselves and the best years of their lives, whether it was a short time or a long time. You probably agree with me that we never have enough time with them. Bear was two weeks away from being sixteen-and-a-half years old. I know that is a very good age, but I still was left wanting more time with her. Sometimes I feel selfish by wishing and wanting that, but I feel this is a normal feeling – never having enough time with them. Even if we had twenty years with them, this would not be enough time. When you love them so deeply, time is never enough.

If we don't move away from the guilt, the guilt will keep us in the grieving process and hold us there. This could lead us into depression, which can be a very dark place to recover from and can be so very debilitating.

I don't have the feeling of guilt. I know deep down in my heart (even though my heart and head were very conflicted) that I made the right decision at exactly the right time. I even had long heart-breaking chats with Bear that I knew she was going to leave me and, although I couldn't bear the thought of her not being here, it was okay for her to go when she was ready. I reaffirmed that she needed to give me a sign.

I had a very long conversation with her and told her I knew she was in pain and we just couldn't make her better, no matter what we did. I explained she would go to the Rainbow Bridge and this place was beautiful but more importantly, there would be no more medications or pain.

Letting go of our pets and saying our goodbyes is the hardest thing in the world. After all, if we need to make that decision, we inadvertently are the ones making that decision of ending their lives. I have never had to make the decision to turn a life support machine off on a person, but that is what I felt I did to Bear – I ended her life. I felt like I had turned her life support machine off. After all, I made the decision on when and how. Sometimes we don't have the opportunity to make that decision, as there are freak accidents or incidents where they get injured and that choice is taken away from us.

In a way, I am glad this wasn't the case with Bear as I got to be there for her very last moment, and got to hold her next to me. I was there when she took her last breath of life. She didn't die an agonising death or on her own. She was surrounded by so much love. I was there right to the very end. I know I did the right thing and I know she would thank me for ending her pain. If she could, she would have thanked me for the very beautiful life I gave her, and the love. She would have told me she loved me, but she would have said, "Thanks for letting me go, Mum, before I suffered."

I think deep in our hearts when we need to make that decision to end our pets' life there is always going to be that element of guilt. At first, I did go through the "What if I had waited a few more days to see if she turned around?" thoughts. Again, there are those 'what ifs'. I had to take the emotion out of it and decide what was best for her – what would Bear expect me to do in her best interest? Would she really want to hang on and be in pain for days?

I knew Bear and the true little fighter that she was. I knew deep in my heart that this was not what she would have wanted. She wouldn't want me to remember her like that. Plus, at the end of the day, I think she deserved so much better than me hanging on to her for my selfish reasons because it was too painful for me to finally say goodbye.

Our pets always had the very best intentions for us and I feel like we need to do the same in return: let them go before the pain becomes too unbearable for them and the suffering too much. I could not and would not let Bear suffer. She didn't deserve that – she gave me the very best years of her life. It was time for me to make that decision and be kind and let her go. It is the hardest decision in the world to make because you know once they go, you cannot bring them back. It is irreversible.

If you are feeling guilt, it is time to let go of that guilt. Our pets would be looking down on us from above and saying to themselves, “Look at what I have done to my mum and dad. I have made them so heartbroken.” Instead, they could be saying, “We had so much love for each other. Now it is time to keep moving forward, remember our love and all of our fond memories.”

I like to try and reassess guilt as follows:

G – Gone but never forgotten
U – Unfair that we have to let go, but they are only ever on loan to us
I – I need to move forward. This is what my pet would want
L – Letting go – It is okay to let go. You will always have the memories, and the love will always be with you. They are still with you in spirit, even if at first you feel like they are not
T – Time to move forward. There is no time limit on this, but look for a purpose – what is going to help you to move forward

There are typically five stages of grief:

1. **Denial**
2. **Anger**
3. **Negotiation**
4. **Depression**
5. **Acceptance**

I know all these so well. The denial: I am still struggling with this one, as I know I am not going to see her again and she really is gone. The anger: I am not feeling angry, as I made the right decision by her to let her go, before she began suffering.

Negotiation: I would use this a lot in my prayers every night. "Please let her stay. I promise I will be a better person."

Depression: I can honestly say I do feel a certain amount of depression –not sleeping or eating and really not wanting to be around people, feeling like I have nothing to look forward to or what is the purpose of continuing and not wanting to celebrate birthdays or even Christmas. Wanting to stay at home, not go out and not do anything is not healthy.

I honestly don't want to be in social scenarios or have social interactions with too many people. I am not ready for that and that is okay. Right now, it isn't about everyone else. Right now, it is about me and what I feel I can cope with. True friends and family are understanding of this. I am very lucky to have an amazing support network around me who will make sure I don't fall, but also understand where I am in life at the moment.

Luckily, I have a lot of friends who don't give me the choice of seeing them or not. They have just been turning up with food and making me eat. Support is one of the biggest things that will help you get through this. Don't be scared to lean on people or be vulnerable with those you can trust. I think acceptance along with denial are two of the hardest stages to get through. Denial is there every day, hoping you will wake up and it just be a bad dream.

When you get to acceptance, I think you have made it through the other side of the grief. It doesn't mean you have forgotten them – it just means you have worked through the other stages, and you are learning to get on with life the best way you can and are beginning to cope a little better each day.

There is another element of guilt some people feel. It is the moment you first laugh or smile at something or enjoy time out with a friend.

You begin to feel guilty; you feel like all of a sudden you are moving away from your pet and getting on with your life. We need to remember it is okay to start moving forward, it is okay to smile and laugh and look forward to things. This is the moment where you are starting the healing process. You don't have to feel guilty about being happy – this is what our pets would want for us. I know, for me, in those moments, Bear would have a smile on her face and be saying to herself, "I am proud of you, Mum."

The love and memories will always be there in your heart and mind. You have photos you can look upon, but more importantly, our hearts will always retain the love and memories. They will travel everywhere and be with you every minute of the day, no matter what you are doing.

The Rainbow Bridge

There are so many beautiful stories about the Rainbow Bridge. It can have different meanings for so many of us. My takeaway, and what I like to think the Rainbow Bridge means is, it's like a stopover for pets before their final destination. I believe they wait for us in this stopover (layover) and wait for us to arrive, so we can enter the next realm together. Once we have arrived, we cross to the other side of the Rainbow Bridge and enter heaven together, never to be parted again.

They wait patiently with love. The bond remains in both their hearts and ours. They watch over us, and continue to love us. They play, enjoy fulfilled health (no more health conditions or medications) and when the time is right for us to be reunited, we join them. I believe we move on to that final destination together. When I think of the Rainbow Bridge this way, it somehow provides me with a level of comfort and puts me at ease. I truly believe we reunite with them when the time is right.

I like to think the Rainbow Bridge is a happy, calm and peaceful place where the sun shines all day long, birds sing, the skies are blue, there are trees for shade, the grass is green and our pets live a happy life. Our beloved pets have crossed and are playing together and feel a rejuvenation of their health. There is no more illness, pain or sickness and no more medications. I know Bear would be waiting at the other side ready to greet all the new pets under her paws, showing them the ropes and reassuring them that everything will be alright. She would be offering comfort.

Bear always had a beautiful nature, welcoming everyone in to her heart and home. She had a reassuring way about her, making you feel like you would be okay and that no matter how hard things seemed, everything would work out. More importantly, she made me feel like I would be okay. They have grown their angel wings and are watching over us, looking forward to seeing us again.

Credit: Author unknown. Fine Art America

There has been many a time when I think that Bear notices when I am feeling sad and upset. I say to friends that I feel like Bear watches over

Credit - Rainbow Bridge picture with dogs and horses - Search (bing.com)

me when I am feeling down. I have always pictured Bear wearing a pair of wings, sitting on a cloud high above the sky over the Rainbow Bridge, looking down on me.

When she is looking down, I feel a wave of comfort and calm, almost like she is saying, "Don't be sad, Mum. I am right here. I know you can't see me, but I know you can feel my presence." I hope that by feeling this way and sharing it, it will provide comfort for someone else.

I believe that even though they leave their physical bodies behind, their spirit remains with us until the time comes for us to be reunited with them again. Even though we feel like they are far away, and at times we feel like they are not with us, they are. I know when I am struggling and ask Bear for signs, she sends just the right sign at the right time that only I would realise.

For example, I was sobbing on the lounge the other night, my heart aching for her. I asked her if she was around, and could she show me a sign. Up came an ad on the television for bubbles. Bear used to love playing bubbles; it was her most favourite game. It was at that moment I smiled and thanked her for sending me that sign. I felt at ease and comforted. This has happened numerous times with butterflies, feathers, and dragonflies.

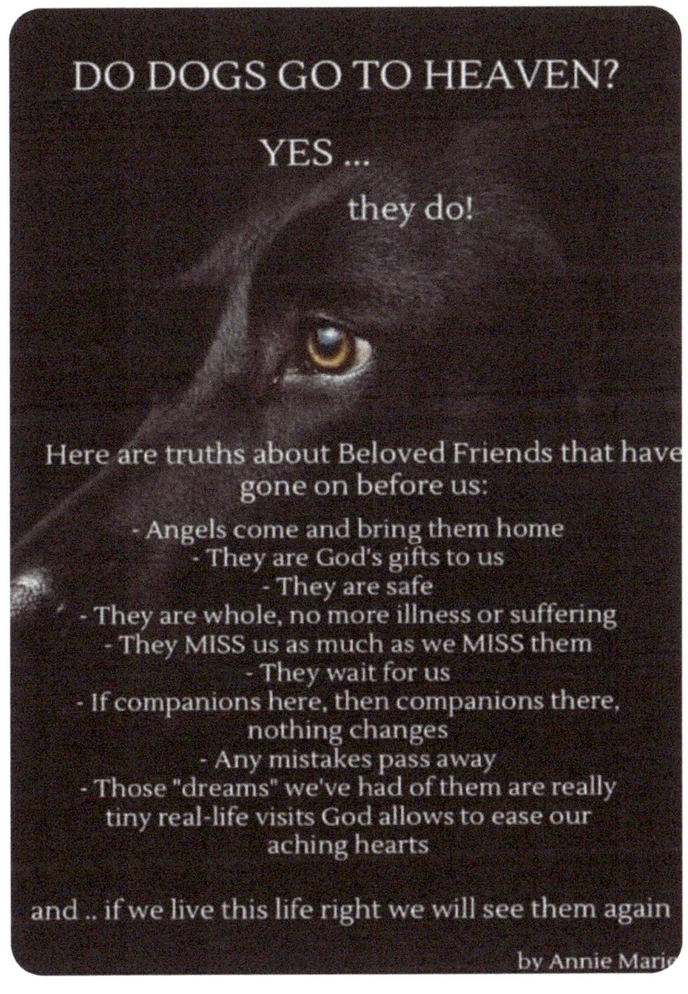

Credit: Lion's Market by Ann (quote by Annie Marie) Photo by Freddie Marriage on Unsplash

My journey

I want to share a little bit about me, to show you where I was in life. I wasn't suicidal but I had given up on myself and the world, and I believed everyone was out to hurt me. To me, this was the way of the world. I wasn't really enjoying life and was a broken-down person who was merely living in a shell. For those of you who have had that pet bond with you, you will understand when I say that animals have a way of healing you, making you a better person. They make you look at the world differently and make you feel better about things you are experiencing in life. They have a way of reaching into your soul and knowing what you need, without you even realising. They can reach out to you in ways most humans can't, not even medical professionals.

As a child growing up, I always had a love for animals and a passion for them. I was a very emotional kid and found myself not being able to watch animal documentaries where animals were being killed (even for survival purposes in the wild). As a very young child, I always wanted to be a vet so I could fix animals and make their lives better. I was a very timid child growing up. I was very trusting of others and seemed to look at the world through rose-coloured glasses, assuming everyone was nice, and I would never be hurt by someone. WOW, what an innocent way of looking at the world, and oh how I was wrong and learnt some very hard, valuable lessons in life.

My turmoil started at the very young age of fourteen in high school, year eight. I was bullied and taunted by a group of six girls. They would push me around, call me names and seem to genuinely get a kick out of bullying me and watching me cry. They would follow me home all the way, taunting me. I would be in tears, and they would push me over on the road. I remember most nights going to sleep crying and wishing I would die and not wake up in the morning.

It got so bad that at one point, one of the girls turned up on the doorstep to my family home to give me a letter. It was on a weekend, and Mum and Dad came to the door and asked the girl what it was. She said some guy around the corner gave it to her and asked her to give it to me. (It is amazing how I remember all the details like it was yesterday. When you have been bullied to such an extent, it is a permanent scar that doesn't heal and you carry it around with you forever. It really can impact the rest of your life and your decision-making.) I opened up the letter, and it was a death threat. The letters had been cut out of a magazine and stuck on with glue and the message read, "You're going to die tonight."

My mum and dad were horrified. We got the police involved, the school principal and even some of these girls' parents. Of course, the parents were in complete denial, stating that their child wouldn't do something like this, and it must be a mistake. I could write all night about this but this book is not my biography.

Needless to say, the bullying continued for another eighteen months to two years. One day, my brother pulled me aside and said, without Mum and Dad knowing, the only way to stop this was to push them back when they pushed me or threw a punch. He said if I didn't start fighting back it would continue. I don't condone violence, but certainly nothing else was working. So, I decided one day in the science lab, I had had enough of being pushed around.

I did just that: I PUSHED BACK. By doing so, I pushed one of them into the science lab's cupboards. The shock on this girl's face was priceless. From that moment on, I still got bullied with the taunting and name-calling, but never got pushed around or tripped over on my way home from school again. I also had a good friend – to this day we are still friends – who used to stick up a lot for me. However, she couldn't be around me all the time as we were in separate classes. I will never forget the way she defended me – she did karate, and the bullies feared her.

I begged Mum and Dad to let me leave school in year nine as the bullying was just too bad. They told me to ignore them, as they would eventually get tired of it and stop (they never did). Eventually, we came to a compromise that if I completed year ten, I could leave and find a job. There went any dreams of being a vet. Bullies don't realise the impact they can make on someone, and how life-altering their actions can be, in some cases causing the person to take their own life. I left school in year ten and did a couple of courses and became a receptionist and worked my way up from secretary to personal assistant to office manager. It took me most of my working life and various certificates/diplomas to get to where I am now.

A couple of years ago, I ran into two of the biggest bullies. One was in a supermarket shopping with her kids. I couldn't help myself. I went up to her, called her by her name and asked her how she was. She replied with, "Do I know you?" I said, "You should remember me. I am the kid you bullied for almost two years at high school and sent me a death threat."

She seemed shocked and said, "What?" I said, "Really? You're going to play that card? You guys made my life a living hell." She was all huffy and said, "I have no idea what you are talking about." Her kids were shocked; they appeared to be in their early teens. I said, "Well, now that you have children of your own, I hope they don't ever have to experience what you put me through."

I ran into the other main bully at her workplace. I had to hand my license over, and she said to me, "I know you, don't I? Did I go to school with you? Your name is familiar." I replied, "Oh yes, you certainly do know me. Is it not ringing a bell yet?" She replied, "Only that I know your name and I went to school with you." I said, "It is so much more than that. You don't remember that poor, shy, quiet girl at school that you bullied and tormented for almost two years and turned up on my doorstep with a death threat? I really hope your memory can't be that bad. I know you have kids of your own. I hope they don't go through anything like what you put me through."

I told her she had changed my life forever. With that, she seemed shocked. She went pale and said she would be back in a minute. With that, she walked over to what I could only assume was her team leader or manager. She walked back with this person and continued to complete my transaction with this person standing right by her side in case I made a scene.

It actually felt good after twenty-six years to be able to look two out of the six bullies in the face and confront them. I am sure my astuteness will play on their minds for many years to come – nothing like what they did to me.

My next life-changing event was at the age of seventeen. In 1992, I was raped. I knew the person, and it was one of the worst experiences of my life. I remember telling them no, and to stop, but that didn't matter to this person. The next day, he said, "If you tell anyone about this or go to the police, it will be my word against yours, not to mention going to court and having people judge you. No one is going to believe you."

I was shocked, devastated, hurt – emotionally and physically – but more importantly, I felt filthy dirty. I felt like I wanted to vomit. He took away my innocence. I kept going over in my head what I had done to give him mixed signals. Had I said the wrong thing? Did I encourage him in the wrong manner? At the end of the day, you can go over it as much as possible but NO means NO.

I had one friend that I told, and she was a great support. She kept encouraging me to go to the police and seek counselling but I just felt too scared, ashamed and embarrassed. The perpetrator got away with it. If I could turn back time, I would have tried to be a stronger person and go to court and the police, but I was too scared that no one would believe me, and I was worried for my parents and how my brothers would react. For quite a while, I was very fearful around men, especially ones I didn't know.

A couple of years later, I met someone at a party who was a friend of a friend. He seemed nice and we started dating, but then things changed. I became more of a possession and not a person. It especially got worse when we moved in together. I was in a domestic relationship for approximately six to nine months. I had bruises where no one would see. I would purposely wear sweaters like skivvies that would cover my neck to hide finger-mark bruising where he would grab me by the throat.

One night, he came home drunk, and we had an argument. He threw me across the dining room table. I managed to grab a pan and hit him with it, which knocked him down. The next day, I remember saying I wanted him to leave and that we were done. Being in a domestic violence relationship is very hard, because they are always apologetic the next day, bringing gifts and promising it will never happen again. You think they can change and the situation will change, BUT it doesn't get any better. The hits get harder and more frequent. Unfortunately, it has to be up to the individual to gain the strength to leave. Nobody can do it for you. Ultimately, you have to be the one to leave. I don't know where I found the courage, but I left this relationship.

In my early twenties, I wanted to be a police officer. I guess you could say all the bad things that had happened to me previously made me want to help others and stop bad people from doing bad things, but I had lost my belief in myself as a person. A couple of years later, I ran off the rails a little. I guess I was rebelling from all the bad experiences. I had disengaged from life and had the attitude that I didn't care. I made myself a promise that no man was ever going to hit or hurt me again. I didn't care who it was. I was going out most nights drinking and partying with my friends. It was at this point I felt like I was living my best life.

At the age of twenty-five, I guess you could say I was in the prime of my life. I had a lot of friends and went partying. I seemed to have no direction in life, but that was okay, as I was happy for the first time in a long time. In May of 2000, I became ill suddenly. I went to the doctor, and she told me I had a stomach virus. She gave me antibiotics, but the following week, I was back at the doctor getting worse. She said she felt it was my appendix and sent me off to the hospital.

I went into the hospital on the Monday morning. The doctors started doing a tonne of tests and said it wasn't my appendix but couldn't find out what was wrong with me. By the Thursday morning, a pain management specialist came to see me about my symptoms. He asked if I had had an endoscopy or colonoscopy. I told him no and explained I didn't even know what that was. He said he would order one and explained it was exploratory, where they would put cameras inside me and look around to see what was going on.

Just after lunch on the Thursday, three days after being in hospital, I was taken for both tests. The next thing I knew, it was Saturday afternoon, and I was waking up in intensive care. I told my nurse I needed to go to the bathroom, but she wouldn't let me out of bed. I had a central line down my neck. I looked at my stomach, and it was like a noughts and crosses board. I said, "What is going on?" My mum and dad were there, and they said I was very sick and needed to rest.

I was scared of what was happening. A specialist doctor came in an hour or two after I woke up, and the first thing he did was abuse me. He said I was a very stupid girl, as I would have known I was sick for some time. At the start of this journey, I was a very shy and quiet girl who had been through some big challenges – some of the worst things that life can throw at you at such a young age.

At twenty-five I started to find my strength as a person, and my voice. I looked at my nurse and told him to get the F&*K out of there and find me another doctor. I said I was not going to be spoken to like that. I had just lost two to three days of my life and he was going to speak to me like that? Nope, I was not putting up with that. They found me another doctor who has been my specialist for the last twenty-two years, and he has been incredible, knowledgeable, understanding, caring and kind. I have complete trust and faith in him and his care of my medical condition.

I have a chronic medical condition called Crohn's Disease, a chronic inflammatory bowel disease which affects the lining of the digestive tract and can sometimes, in severe cases, cause life-threatening complications and death. Some patients require multiple surgeries and end up with a bag. I have to be careful what I eat and drink. I don't smoke or drink alcohol, only very occasionally. I am on long-term medication. Crohn's is reactive to stress – they even call it a stress-related condition. At times, when I have had chronic flare-ups, I have been bedridden, taking around twenty-eight tablets a day, all of which fight each other. I become a prisoner in my own home, as I can't leave the house due to accidents. I guess you could say I coped really well during lockdown – isolation and being housebound was no stranger to me.

I spent the first two years between the ages of twenty-five and twenty-seven in and out of hospital, as I wasn't managing my condition well. I hadn't worked out what my triggers were, and I wasn't managing the medications very well. One of the medications is a steroid called prednisone which can have pretty serious side effects, especially on higher dosages to control the bleeding and inflammation. I am now forty-six, and due to the long term use of the steroids, I am close to developing osteoporosis.

One day, I said to my mum, "I am so young. Why me? Poor me." My mum said it was okay to have a pity party and feel like that, but that I couldn't stay in that place. I couldn't unpack and live there. She gave me strength to keep pushing on and told me to make the disease learn to live with me, not to live with it.

My mum has always been my strength through this journey – my rock. She would sit at my bedside morning and night, always encouraging me to look forward to things and plan things. She said I was one of the strongest people she knows. I have, over the years, tried to build a strong, healthy mind and diet. My specialist believes this strong mindset is what helps to keep me in remission with the illness.

Fast-forward a few years to when I was thirty years old. Not only had I endured all of that (I had overcome it and dug deep), but life was not yet finished throwing curve balls at me just yet.

My next life-changing moment was when I was thirty. One of my brothers attacked me in front of witnesses. I was assaulted in the kitchen, pushed into a corner kitchen cupboard and grabbed around the throat. The pressure became so intense, I could feel myself struggling to breathe. The people around just froze in sheer shock. Only when I started to gasp for breath did his girlfriend jump in and grab him off me. He let go of me and said, "You're lucky you're not in a body bag." You never in a million years think a family member is going to aggressively assault you.

Due to the family dynamics, I am not allowed to divulge any more of this matter, other than to say I was only able to place an AVO on this person. Another family member had threatened me to prevent this brother from being charged. This was a very big turning point in my life. Not only did it cause much family upheaval and even ruin family relationships, but it was the point where I said no man was going to put a hand on me again, and once again, I was forced into a situation where I was held back from charging this brother.

I only wish to this day I went against my family member's threat and had him charged and held him accountable for what he did. He has gone on to reoffend and had a further AVO placed on him from another family member. He also attacked another person in the same way he attacked me around the throat but has always gotten away with this behaviour.

It was at this point I started to find belief in myself and tell myself that if I want to be a police officer, medical condition and all, I was going to have to fight hard. I applied and was knocked back a couple of times for various reasons, but I wasn't taking no for an answer. This was a turning point in my life. I was sick of being everyone's doormat and being treated like garbage. I was now becoming a bigger, better stronger version of myself. I was done. I was done being a victim and was done having bad things happen to me. More importantly, I believe my life experiences were vital in helping others.

I applied at the age of thirty-two and got another knock back due to my lack of study, as I hadn't studied for fifteen or so years. Academically, I needed to show I could handle this component of the course. I went back to TAFE and studied a Cert IV in Small Business Management two nights a week for a year.

I reapplied and got in. I completed nine months of the course and failed leading into my last few months to graduation. I got sick with gastro, which then triggered a Crohn's flare. I was out for three months and could go back but had to repeat part of the course. I took this failure pretty hard and chose not to go back. It's one of my biggest regrets to this day.

At the age of thirty-five, I moved to a very remote location – an indigenous community in a very small town called Goodooga about ten hours from Sydney, with my partner at the time. I moved away from work, family and friends and my medical team. The things you do for love! At this time, Bear was five years old, and we had Angel, her partner in crime – a little foxy Chihuahua which I will talk more about later.

During our time in this small town, we got engaged and also had two miscarriages. It was so debilitating being away from family and friends and all the things I knew. We were in a town which only had a small pub, school, and post office. We made friends whilst out there, but it wasn't home. It was a means to a bigger, brighter future. We bought twenty-five acres at Mudgee, a beautiful country town approximately three hours from Sydney (still close enough but far enough away).

I found it very challenging at first living in a remote country town, as I was a city girl through and through, but sometimes you have to throw the gauntlet down and get out of your comfort zone. Getting out of your comfort zone can be one of the most frightening but exhilarating experiences. If you embrace change, it can be one of the most exciting experiences, opening new doors and new chapters along with new people.

During my second pregnancy, I went for our twelve-week scan and they couldn't find a heartbeat. My heart felt like it was about to stop beating, and I felt like I was dying inside. It was one of the worst feelings ever, hearing those words – we can't find a heartbeat.

As we were in a country town, I was in denial. The sonographer rang my specialist obstetrician in Penrith NSW (I don't think he wanted to tell us the bad news).

My obstetrician spoke with us and said we need to come back home ASAP, as she said the last measurement that could be seen for the foetus was ten-and-a-half weeks. She said to come back home, and that she would do an intensive scan in her room, and if all was correct, she would need to do a curette. She said she would book the hospital just in case, as she knew how far away we were living. She was amazing. She had organised everything. It is not often you come across medical professionals who are caring and kind but have impeccable, supportive bedside manners.

We arrived in her rooms, and she did the scan and confirmed I had lost the baby at ten-and-a-half weeks and that we would need to go to hospital to do the curette. She removed all the tissue and took about fourteen tubes of blood to test for everything imaginable. We had to go back to the country two days later, but I was not ready to go back and leave my friends and family. However, my ex-fiancé had to get back for work. Needless to say, I was completely and utterly devastated. I had dreamed of having my own family, and I really wanted children. I knew my pregnancies would be high-risk due to my Crohn's and medications, but never thought I would go through this.

The obstetrician rang us a week later to tell us she had more bad news. With the tissue sample she took, she explained I'd had a partial molar pregnancy and wouldn't have carried past about fourteen weeks. A partial molar pregnancy is an abnormal pregnancy in which the embryo develops incompletely. She went on to explain that if she didn't remove all the tissue, I could get cancer of the stomach and in other areas. If that was the case, I would need a round of chemo.

In the meantime, I had to have blood tests every Friday for six months, and then drop to every fortnight for a year, to make sure the HCG levels were dropping. If they rose or they didn't drop, this could be an indicator of cancer. I also had to have chest and abdomen X-rays every two months for a year. After that year, I would get the all-clear if everything during that time was normal. Then we would be able to try again but would need close monitoring through the next pregnancy.

Just when I thought life had thrown enough at me, I had to go through this. As you can imagine, I was completely devastated. I was in a remote location with no family or friends for support, and my partner told me to get on with life and get back to work and that we could try again once we got the all-clear. But he didn't understand the feelings and emotions. After all, it wasn't his body going through this turmoil or transformation.

I wasn't in a good headspace. I had found a lot of trees which I was going to run the car into. He often found me curled up in the bedroom or shower in a foetal position. I just wasn't coping and didn't know how to move on from this. I honestly thought I had been through everything in life and that there was nothing more that could be thrown at me. I went to a psychologist for two sessions but didn't find it useful. I understand they go to university and study for a variety of things, but I believe sometimes the best person to help you is someone who has walked in your shoes.

But this is where the story takes an even sadder turn. Six months after the loss of a second pregnancy, while I still wasn't clear from all the medical tests, my now ex-fiancé showed interest in his work colleague, and I was basically told to pack my stuff and go. Adding more insult to injury, this other woman sent me a text message asking if I would like a hand organising a removalist – really.

How does one continue from this amount of heartbreak in one short lifetime? I look back, and I honestly can't tell you how I survived. I think it is exactly like what I am doing now with the loss of Bear – one small step at a time, day by day, crying whenever I feel like it. But, on reflection, I look at everything I have been through, and I am still here. They say tough times don't last, but tough people do. I guess I am a living, breathing testament of this. I must be Tonka tough by now.

In the meantime, while we were in this remote location, I found a horse – or should I say, he found me. He was a beautiful palomino whom I named Sunny, because every time I saw him, he made me smile from ear to ear. Unfortunately, I had to leave him behind and give him away. This broke my heart, as he and I had bonded. I was reunited with him two-and-a-half years ago. His owner asked if I would like him back. He was not in a good way at all, but now he is living a lovely retirement with me and living a great life as every horse should.

I had a heart full of hurt, grief, disappointment and sorrow. When I first met Bear, I knew she would impact my life, but didn't realise how much. Within a very short period of time, it was like she had a key to my heart. With this key, she released the hurt. The scars were still there and will always be there, but my heart was now opening. She showed me love, laughter, companionship, but most of all she showed me how to live life, be brave and resilient. I am the person I am today because of one small fur baby called Bear – a Jack Russell who was small in stature but had a big heart and was larger than life.

I moved back home to my parents completely broken, distraught and in such a mess. I had no idea where to go from there, what to do or how the hell I was going to pick myself up. I stayed with Mum and Dad for five weeks, then found a rental property with Bear, Angel and Puss. I didn't work for a few months, as I was debilitated by grief, depression, hurt and anger.

This is where Bear saved my life

April 2014, on a rainy Sunday afternoon. Leading up to this day I had been researching ways to take my life. I had decided to fill up the bath and drop a hairdryer into it and electrocute myself. I had been planning it for a couple of weeks but never had the courage until this day.

I was in the deepest, darkest point in my life. I was in true despair. I honestly believed the pain was too great for me to overcome and there was nothing more for me to look forward to – I felt like my life was truly over. I wanted the pain to end, and this was the only way to stop the pain.

I hope that by sharing my journey, this will provide others with hope and inspiration. If I can be a survivor and overcome these challenges, others can find the courage to overcome their own challenges too. I am not saying it was easy – everything that I have been through was extremely tough and soul-destroying – but if you can dig deep, you can come out the other side. It takes courage and also support from friends, but most of all it takes determination and hard work. If you work hard, you can build resilience and become a better person. It is extremely hard to find positives from negatives, but if you can do that, you will become a bigger, better version of yourself.

At the time I lost Bear, I could see nothing positive – after all, I had lost my world. However, once again, as Bear always did, she left me with a purpose. I hope this book helps provide courage, support and comfort for others. She also left me with her legacy, which is now for me to fight and become an advocate for pets and other pet parents.

When our pets are part of our lives, they give us a purpose. We feel like we can take on any challenge, as they are right by our side. They make us face the world and face the hard days because we know they are by our side. When I lost Bear, I felt like my purpose in life had gone. It actually hadn't – it was still there – I just couldn't see it due to the grief. We need to look beyond the grief and find that purpose. Just because we lose our pets doesn't mean our purpose is gone. Having a purpose is a reason for you to keep pushing on, and this will help you move through the stages of grief.

How Bear and I met and how she changed my life

I was looking for a while to get a pup. I knew I wanted a Jack Russell. I had read up about them and knew they had a full-of-life, quirky little personality that was sassy and just full of go, go, go – just what I needed. It was a Thursday night in the last week of July 2005. I had noticed a white Jack Russell pup at a pet store in Campbelltown about a forty-minute drive from my home. I rang the store, and they advised the pup was still available, and it was a little girl who was nine weeks old. I said I would love to come in and see her, and that I particularly wanted her. They said they would hold her until Saturday afternoon, so I left my details and even offered to leave a deposit. They said that wasn't necessary.

On the Friday night, I had been out celebrating my thirtieth birthday and celebrated a little too hard and woke up the Saturday morning slightly hungover. My mum and dad offered to take me to see the puppy, as I was living with them at the time. Mum suggested I call to make sure the puppy was still available before we drove all the way over there, and to let them know we were coming. When I rang, I was told that they sold her the day before. I was pretty upset. I was sure she was the right one for me. Low and behold, the universe had other plans.

My dad suggested we take a trip out to Kellyville Pets. He said they usually have a good range of pets, and always had puppies. We took a drive out to Kellyville Pets about a half-hour drive from my house. We arrived and there were these three precious Jack Russells – a boy and two girls. Bear's brother and sister were pretty full-on at the glass; they seemed very boisterous. I asked the lady if I could hold the one at the back and that I was wanting to buy a puppy. I had no names picked out prior and said to Mum the name would come to me when I held the pup.

Well, I held Bear. She licked me and had the happiest, waggiest of tails. She was just full of joy and excitement. I told Mum this was the one for me. I said "Mum, meet Bear. Bear, meet Nan and Pop." That was it. We got her toys and food and commenced our journey home. I was nursing her in the back seat, when suddenly I felt a rush of sickness come over me. I said to my dad, "You will need to pull over, I'm going to be sick."

With that, Dad pulled over and I passed Bear to my mum in the passenger seat. I got out the car and threw up, and as I threw up, Bear threw up all over my mum. Mum said it was almost simultaneous. Bear had obviously been given Weetbix at the pet store for breakfast. I got back in the car, and Mum said Bear was eager to get back to me. Mum said it was almost like Bear knew I was her mum. Mum had always said to me from this very first day and the moment we were both sick at the same time, that Bear was in tune with me and it was

like we were one. I felt that way too. Bear always knew if I was happy, sad or sick. She knew everything about me – all the cues possible. She was pretty remarkable, to be honest.

My dad was always very strict about pets. He didn't believe in pets being in the house or on furniture. He said Bear could come in at night but strictly had to sleep in the laundry.

The first three nights, Bear cried and cried and cried, no matter what we did. I had a beautiful soft bed and blankets, and it was warm in the laundry; we had ducted heating and cooling through the house. We had newspaper down for her to do her business, and a clock, as I was told this would replicate the mother's heartbeat.

After three nights of badly interrupted sleep, Mum, Dad and I were so sleep-deprived (it was like having a baby in the house), I decided on night four I would sneak into the laundry after Mum and Dad had gone to bed and bring her into my bed. Let's just say from that moment on, that is where Bear slept – in my bed with me. She was the perfect cuddle buddy.

Needless to say, Bear took over the house. My dad fell in love with her, and Bear had the run of the home inside and out. Bear was amazing to toilet train. I think she was fully toilet trained in less than two weeks and had only very few accidents in the house. She would alert us by running to the back door or by sitting at our feet, barking and nudging us with her nose. If she seemed pacy I would ask her if she wanted to go to the toilet. If so, she would run to the back door. She was honestly the perfect puppy.

Bear went to puppy preschool, and the trainer said she was such a distraction to the class. She had a mind of her own and she would definitely use it. She was so much like me – courageous, independent and headstrong. Although she was amazingly smart and easy to train, if she didn't want to do something, there was no getting her to do it. She thrived on praise and treats, and even right up until her last few days on earth, she would still devour her treats.

Bear had the most courageous, outgoing personality. She was fearless – she loved chasing birds and butterflies and hunting for lizards. I bought her a sandpit and she used to dig until her heart was content. I would bury toys and treats in there. She was such a playful little girl. When Mum was sweeping, she would attack the broom and try and pull it out of Mum's hands. Not to mention the vacuum – she hated it. She wasn't scared, but would try and attack it. She made household chores so much more fun.

Her favourite game was bubbles. I used to buy doggy-friendly bubbles, and she would run around popping them. If I said, "Bear, do you want to play bubbles?" she would go to the cupboard where they were kept and sit there barking to say, "Come on, hurry up."

As Bear grew, so did our bond. She became more and more in tune with my Crohn's Disease, and she could tell I was sick before I started showing symptoms. She would pick up on my mood and the way I was feeling and was always there to comfort me. If I was vomiting in the toilet, she was right there next to me looking up at me with big brown eyes, waiting for me to reassure her I was alright. I once asked my vet how she knew I was sick before I showed symptoms. Was it something she just sensed? The vet explained that when you're well and you kiss and cuddle them, they get use to your saliva smelling a particular way, but when you get sick, your saliva changes. This was obviously how Bear was picking up my sickness before I started to show symptoms.

Bear wasn't a pet or a dog, she was my child – a true companion and therapy girl. Crohn's can be very debilitating, isolating and depressing, but she always knew how I was feeling and knew exactly how to make me feel better and laugh. When I was sick, she never, ever left my side. She brought me so much comfort and such that I'd never gotten from too many people. In fact, I had lost friends along the way because they didn't understand my illness or why I had to cancel last-minute plans. She had a way of reaching me on levels that no one else could. With her by my side, it didn't matter how bad I felt. I would be okay because she was always there, and between the two of us, we could take on the world.

When I had Crohn's flare, I would be bedridden for days at a time. Bear would lie right by my side, either up near my neck, or laying her head on my chest, almost saying to me, "Mum, I am listening to your heartbeat." Much later in life, when I started needing iron infusions due to my iron being low, she would start to sniff and lick the back of my right hand almost as much as to say, "Mum, it is about time you got an iron top up." I would go to the doctor and he would do a blood test, and sure enough my iron would be low and I would need an iron infusion.

After I had the iron infusion, I would come home and she would sniff the back of my hand as if to say, "Good, you've had it done. Now let's play." I believe Bear and I were so in tune, she could read my thoughts, and we would speak to each other, not necessarily through words, but our eyes. Bear was always a very hyperactive, full-on playful character, even up until the last two months of her life. She would play so actively with her little sister, Angel, and at times outplay her. Bear had such quirks. I would make her bed every night so nice and neat and she would get in there and scrunch it up into a ball and then lie on it as if to say, "Mum, I don't like the way you make my bed."

She didn't like being dressed up, but loved bathtime. She would stand still in the bath and move her neck and back as if to say, "Scratch me here, Mum." Boy, when she got out of the bath, she had a mad attack of the zoomies, and nothing and no one could stop her. She would have me and anyone else visiting in absolute fits of hysterics. She would even get this growl going – I use to call it her motor. This brings a slight smile to my face when I remember our precious memories.

She was such a great eater. She would eat everything apart from mashed potato, but she loved ice cream, McDonald's chicken nuggets, red frogs, packets of chips, and even knew exactly where they were kept in the cupboards and fridge. She always wanted what I was eating. The last year of her life, she became very fussy. She would sit in front of me waiting for handouts, and when I finished my dinner, she would give me the evil eye and walk off slowly as if to say, "Well, I better go and eat my dinner now, since you are not going to share your dinner."

Bear's vocabulary was out of this world. She knew words like car, mum, nan, pop, chips, frogs, ice cream, Angel, ball, lizards, bed, walkies, walk, birdies, Mr. Puss, Sunny and even my friends' names. Mum and Dad had nicknames for me like Jo or Joey, and if I was out and rang in to see if they needed anything on the way home, or to see how Bear was, or just to let them know I was on the way home, she just seemed to know it was me. She would run to the door and sit and wait. Mum said it was beautiful to watch. Let's not even mention the excitement – she would act like I had been away for months. There is a true saying – we have friends and family and work and go out, but for our pets we are all they have.

She knew her vet, Michelle, and if I said to Bear, "Are you going to see Michelle?" she would run to the laundry to get her lead and run to the front door barking. When we got to the vet's she would walk in – or should I say trot (she had this little trot like a horse) – almost to say, "Hi fans, I am here." Everyone at the vet practice loved her, and she loved them. She was always happy to go to the vet's and see them all. I videoed Bear one night while I was talking about the vet Michelle and sent it to her. We couldn't say words at home, so we had to start spelling them out. I remember many a night she would be asleep on the lounge. Yes, that's right, she was allowed on the furniture and she even spent some nights in my mum and dad's bed if I was away.

Bear had my mum and dad wrapped around her little paw. My dad would say, "I might go and get a packet of C H I P S." (That's right, he would spell it out rather than say the word.) Bear would be fast asleep on the lounge, he would sneak out to the kitchen and grab the chips, but little did he know he had a stalker right behind him. She would stare at him, quietly waiting for him to turn around with the chips, as if to say, "Did you honestly think you were going to sneak a packet of chips and not share?" Gee, she made us laugh a LOT. She filled our hearts with so much love, joy and happiness.

Wherever she went, she lit up a room. Everybody loved her and she loved everyone. She didn't have a mean or aggressive streak in her body. She had this way of touching everyone's lives and hearts. My mum would often say she had been to earth before – that she was reincarnated, a person in fur. People couldn't believe how interactive she was and how much she knew. She was full of love and had so much love to give, and her eyes … she had a way of talking to you and communicating with her eyes and her bark.

When I was thirty-two, my niece was born. My mum had my niece from about four months old, Monday to Friday. My mum and dad had a full nursery set up for her. When Mum put my niece down for her midday nap, Bear would stay in the nursery and lie next to the cot on the floor, while my niece slept. If my niece stirred or woke up, Bear would go find my mum in the house to let her know the little one was awake.

When I met Bear, I was a broken-down person, but Bear almost resuscitated me. She brought me back to life. Bear gave me so many things in life, so much love and laughter – I had almost forgotten how to laugh and truly enjoy life. She also provided me with strength, courage and resilience. I finally found direction and purpose in life. She gave me the belief back in myself. She made me feel like I was ten feet tall and bulletproof. I could do anything because of Bear; the tough days were easier because of her. The most important part of my journey with Bear made me whole again. She helped me in ways that medical professionals or medications couldn't. This is the empowerment of true love and the bond with a pet. It is magical and creates a feeling of euphoria.

How Bear saved my life

Back to that dark day in April 2014. I had the hairdryer plugged in and switched on. I stood up in the bath, and it was literally about two to three seconds before I was ready to drop the hairdryer into the water, when all three of my pets – Bear, Angel and Puss – came rushing in. It was like Bear had gathered the troops for an intervention.

I remember all three of them came in, sat on the mat and stared at me in disbelief of what I was about to do. I stared back at them, and I could read Bear's expression and eyes (as I mentioned previously, Bear use to speak to me with her eyes). It was like they were saying, "This isn't fair. You can't leave us, who will love us and look after us?" Keep in mind, Puss never really got along with Bear and Angel.

He tolerated them, but they were by no means the best of friends. But here they were sitting on the mat side by side in unison. Bear was in the middle, Puss was on Bear's right side as you looked at her and Angel was on Bear's left. I stood there for what felt like a lifetime just staring at them and sobbing (I would say about two minutes). I turned the hairdryer off and dropped it on the ground outside the bath.

Puss walked off as if to say, "My job here is done." He can be such a funny fellow at times – not really a smoocher. I sat back in the bath

– I have no idea how long for, but the water got colder and my skin was all shrivelled. I just sobbed and sobbed and sobbed. I couldn't stop. The whole time while I was in the bath, Angel and Bear sat watching my every move. Angel eventually lay down on the bath mat, but Bear sat there still like a statue, staring at me.

I eventually got out of the bath, took myself into my bedroom, lay on the floor in the foetal position and cried and cried. I remember Bear and Angel leaning up against me as if to say, "It will be alright, we are here with you, we have your back." I know it was late by the time I fed them that night – they were both off their food and obviously stressed because of my distress.

Don't ever believe or let anyone tell you that animals don't know. They do know, and they know more than people give them credit for. If you are reading this and you are the sort of person I am and are truly bonded with your pets, you will understand wholeheartedly what I mean by this statement.

I honestly believe to this day, if it wasn't for Bear especially, but also Puss and Angel, I would have taken my life and wouldn't be here today writing this.

I woke up the next morning, and that was the first day of the rest of my life. I woke up thinking he was not worth that. No pain was worth that, and I needed to pick myself up and get on with life. Since my split with my ex-fiancé more than eight and a half years ago, I have had two short-term relationships. I have trust issues – not just with men, but with people in general, but I knew I needed to find myself and do a lot of soul-searching and deep work on myself to repair the hurt and damage. I can honestly say, leading up to Bear's passing, I was in a good place in my life. I was stronger, more courageous, independent and I realised my own self love and self-worth, which is really important. Before you can love someone else or someone can love you, you have to love yourself and know your own worth.

As I mentioned previously, I believe all our pets are sent to us for a reason. Bear was sent to me to make me a more resilient person, to open up my heart again after it had shut down from so many bad experiences. She showed me what true love and loyalty is like, she showered me with compassion and trust and she made me a more courageous and fearless person who started to feel whole again. I became very resilient and almost fearless. I felt like I could take on the world. She showed me how to be brave, and what it took to be brave and face up to my fears.

Bear was sent to me when I was a broken-down shell of a person who was merely existing in a world and society that seemed so cruel. Nothing can ever repair the damage and scars I carry from my lifetime of bad experiences, but she did make me move on in a more positive way. She brought laughter and happiness into my world, which at times seemed so dull and unhappy, and no matter what I was facing, I always felt like I could take on the world with her by my side. She made me realise I needed to look forward and not look back. After all, you can't change the past, but you can change and create a better future for yourself.

I became a happier, more content person because of Bear. In time, I slowly started to open my heart again and trust people on my terms, letting only selected people in. No matter how bad my Crohn's got, she was right there by my side. Her unwavering devotion and love gave me a reason to keep getting up in the morning and face the crap days. Bear has been through some of my toughest times and having her right there by my side was sheer comfort. I don't think any counsellor, psychologist or psychiatrist would have been able to help me overcome my challenges in life like she did.

Pets are the best medicine and therapy. They get you, they understand you, they heal you and they provide therapy. More importantly, they love you one hundred per cent unconditionally. They don't care if you wake up having a bad hair day, or you didn't brush your hair or didn't have your morning coffee. They only care that you are there and that you love them.

They are always the same. You leave the house to go to work, you come home and you have the happiest, loving welcome home. You have only been gone a day, but to them it feels like a lifetime. Pets are better than humans. We humans could learn so many beautiful traits from pets, such as loyalty, love, compassion, trust and my favourite, faithfulness. Bear has been more faithful to me and kinder than any of my ex partners.

Take a look at how incredible our pets are. We have guide dogs who assist the visually impaired, and we have dogs who are trained to watch over children who have breathing difficulties. They assist people with mental health issues and anxiety. There are pet therapy dogs who go and visit sick kids in hospital and the elderly in nursing homes. Look at our police dogs, for instance, who are trained to track down criminals. We have horses and dogs that are used to assist and help people with PTSD rebuild their lives. I believe they are true heart-healers. Bear gave me a constant purpose every day and still does.

As hard as this journey of grief has been, I know Bear is looking down on me and telling me every day to keep pushing forward, keep putting one foot in front of the other and that there is more for me to achieve on earth. I know she would want me to succeed, and for that, I am going to do her proud. Bear may have passed over to the Rainbow Bridge, but she is still giving me a purpose – this book. Bear would want me to help others and stand up and be a voice, an advocate, for other pets and people. Hopefully this is what this book will achieve. Pets don't want us to give up on life. Bear gave me all the tools I need to be a better, stronger and more resilient person. I am going to strive and continue to kick goals because of her. I am going to beat the grief. I am going to provide a legacy to Bear, and I am very thankful every day that I got to share my life with a fur baby such as her. It was an absolute privilege that she picked me to be her human fur mum.

It is my belief that pets almost have a sixth sense, like this telepathic vision of what we need and when we need it. What do I mean by this? When you and your pet are one, and so in tune with each other, and that bond is so undeniably strong, they know you so well. They know when you are sick, upset, stressed or when you're just not on your game. They know when we need that hug or to bring on their silliness in the hope it will make you smile and laugh. Pets are the best medicine. For instance, if we look at therapy dogs who go and visit sick kids in hospital and the elderly in nursing homes, just by walking in the door, they bring smiles to everyone's face, and hearts melt. These dogs are calm, patient and kind. They provide hugs and make some of the sickest kids come to life with a just a simple visit.

Horses are used for PTSD (Post Traumatic Stress Disorder). They will form a bond with a stranger and look deep into their soul and know what that person needs which is love and support. My horse Sunny has this ability. I know this because everyone he meets feels he is calm and cuddly, but he has patience and kindness. Sunny can be cheeky, playful and calm, depending on my mood. When I lost Bear, I didn't see Sunny for a week and a half. The following week when I saw Sunny, it was Sunday and it was raining heavily. I walked over to him, and I was already crying by the time I reached him. He stood there and looked me dead in the eye. I knew he could feel my pain.

I wrapped my arms around him, sobbing uncontrollably, and told him we had lost sissy Bear. I said there was nothing we could do; it was her time to grow her wings. After I had said the last word, Sunny rested his head on my shoulder and almost pulled me in with his head close to his shoulder and wrapped his head around my shoulders as if to say, "I've got your heavy heart and heavy body." We both stood there motionless for a good ten minutes. I was completely drenched, but I know he knew my exact depth of pain and heartache. He walked with me back to the gate and watched me get in the car and drive away.

I have had children as young as four and five around Sunny, brushing him while he just stood there and went to sleep. I have had a friend around him who was terrified of horses, and had never been around a horse before. She left with a totally different perspective. Don't get me wrong, horses can hurt you, but not because they mean to – they are actually very gentle souls. A horse can be dangerous when spooked or mishandled. Even though I trust Sunny one hundred per cent and I know he trusts me, there is still that element of caution to be exercised in case he became spooked.

Pets and animals have the purest and kindest of souls. They give you all of themselves, they don't hold back and they are always at their happiest when they are with you. The human race really could learn a lot from animals. It is such a shame, as humans we don't take the time out to learn and adopt more of their qualities. I say it all the time: give me animals and pets over people any day of the week.

Bear's medical issues and the last two years

Over the years, Bear had many medical issues, and either overcame them, or we were able to manage them with medication and vet monitoring. She truly was inspirational, and astounded me with just how much she overcame. As a very young pup, Bear had serious allergies. At first, there were many trips to the vet's and we tried many things from dog washes to steroids to antihistamines and creams. Bear's allergies were so bad sometimes, she would bleed and come out in big welts all over her belly and under her armpits.

Finally, the vet suggested we see a doggy dermatologist. She was fantastic. She did quite a lot of allergy testing and suggested we go right back to the basics with food. For approximately six weeks, we had to do a rabbit and rice diet and slowly start introducing foods back into her diet. Once we could see an allergy, we knew that would be the food she was allergic to. By doing the allergy testing we found she was allergic to Kikuyu grass, dog shampoos, and also the changing of the seasons seemed to flare her up. With our lawns, we always had to have them regularly mowed and kept very short. The dermatologist suggested we use Malasab shampoo, which really helped her.

I bathed her twice a week in summer to help with the allergies, and at least fortnightly in winter. She got use to the hairdryer at a young age. At first, she tried to attack it, and it would take my mum to hold her while I used the hairdryer, but then she slowly got used to it.

Bath time would give her a serious attack of the zoomies. Sometimes I think she thought she was superdog – all she needed was a cape. Her allergies took many years of maintenance and control, but as she got a lot older, she seemed to grow out of them. She had very sensitive skin in her early days, but when she got to the age of about ten, her allergies didn't seem to be a problem anymore.

Bear had a couple of late-night emergency trips to the vets. I swear I don't know how I didn't have a heart attack at times with her. I know she kept me on my toes constantly with worry and stress. One emergency vet trip was at around ten p.m. I was getting ready for a night out and had a can of Impulse deodorant on the bed. While I was in the bathroom getting ready, Bear jumped up onto the bed and chewed on the can of deodorant and punctured it in multiple places.

I came back into the bedroom and saw she was vomiting, panting and shaking. She didn't look well at all. My dad drove me to Baulkham Hills Vet (after-hours practice) about half an hour away from our house. The vet checked her over, and by the time we got there, she seemed to be as bright as a button. The vet gave her something for the nausea, checked her temperature and said she could develop some diarrhoea. I had to monitor her for the night, and if I had any concerns, I could ring them back or take her to my own vet the next morning. Needless to say, I didn't end up going out that night. I stayed home with her and watched her like a hawk. After all, she was my baby.

At the next emergency vet visit, she had chronic diarrhoea. She was off her food and vomiting, and she felt very hot and lethargic. I knew Bear so well and knew when something was wrong. I took her to the vet near me. They did some bloods, which came back showing pancreatitis. She stayed in the vet's for forty-eight hours on drips, and they gave her anti-nausea injections. Bear certainly kept me broke with the number of vet visits and surgeries, but I wouldn't have it any other way, and would do it all over again for her or any of my other pets. You cannot put a price on unconditional love.

By the time Bear was about eight years old, she had a luxating patella (loose knee cap). We tried monitoring it but it only got worse. The vet suggested surgery, which cost almost three thousand dollars, and we needed to keep her quiet from four to ten weeks depending on how well everything went and healed. Anyone who owns a Jack Russell knows when a vet tells you to keep them quiet, it is like mission impossible.

(You can hear the *Mission Impossible* tune playing in your head.) You know you have to accept the mission but you have no idea how you are going to do it (LOL). Bear had the surgery, and she came through it with flying colours. We always had trust from day one, but Bear needed to rely on and trust me more than ever.

I took four weeks off work and lay in the lounge room on an air mattress with her to make sure she didn't walk around. I had to put her lead on every time I took her to the toilet, and carry her out and let her walk once we got out on the grass. Keeping Bear quiet was so hard. She was always full of life, like someone had her constantly plugged into a charger.

After eight weeks, the surgery and her bones had healed so well that the metal components started to stick out of the side of the knee. The vet suggested we go back in and remove the metal components as she had healed well.

Once again, the surgery went well, and it wasn't long before Bear was running around like nothing had happened. She would often lift her leg like it was sore, but I knew it wasn't, as she had constant check-ups. I think it was more of a habit, so I got very used to saying to her, "Use your leg." She would turn and look at me as if to say, "Oh, that's right, there is nothing wrong with my leg." She was such a character. There was never a dull moment with her.

About another year after surgery, Bear had another bout of pancreatitis. This wasn't as bad as the first episode she had. Bear's next battle was at the age of eleven. She blew her cruciate ligament in the same leg. Surgery was recommended, which they did, and it was slightly more complicated, as she had scar tissue from her luxating patella surgery. Once again though, Bear came through with flying colours. I wish I could say the same about my bank account taking another three thousand dollar hit. She recovered a little slower but made a full recovery, and in no time was running around like nothing had ever happened. She honestly blew me away with how she took everything in her stride. She was just so brave and resilient.

Bear always showed resilience and recovered well. She knew her own limits, but more importantly, she never complained. She always had a happy disposition and a waggy tail which spoke volumes. Her bravery and courage left me in awe. She gave me so much strength to overcome my own hurdles and obstacles. Bear then had more surgery to remove teeth. In fact, over the years, from age twelve to fifteen, I think she had three lots of surgeries almost yearly, to clean and remove teeth. After the last tooth surgery she had at fifteen, she came home okay, but developed some complications. She wouldn't take her medication and had to have another three days in vet care to get her back on the road to recovery.

It was then suggested I start brushing her teeth. Wow what a battle royale that was. You could do almost anything to Bear, and she would take it in her stride, but whatever you do, don't touch her front paws or brush her teeth. She would fight you to the endth degree not to have her teeth brushed. She would lock her jaw and put your arms in a wrist lock with her little paws. Sometimes I would have to pin her down. Towards the end, it was so stressful brushing her teeth.

In the last two years of Bear's life, she got sick, and we had to do a lot of tests. She started with what was thought to be heart issues or seizures. She had a heart murmur. From memory, a grade two or three. Bear would have these night-time attacks which not only scared me, but made me terrified for her experiencing them. She would collapse, shake, her eyes would roll to the top of head and most times she was completely limp, like she had passed away. Most of the time, I couldn't feel her heart beating. I live on my own and was terrified. Don't ask me how I managed to stay calm, but I knew I needed to be for her.

I would lay her on the ground or hold her and lightly shake her, calling her name. I would clench my fist and rub her chest really quickly with slight pressure. This would last anywhere from one to two minutes, but it felt like a lifetime. When she came to, she would look at me, swaying like she was drunk and confused, so I would just sit with her and talk to her. Within another minute or two, she would stand up and start to wag her tail but would be very lethargic for the next twenty-four hours.

The vet suggested we see a specialist heart cardiologist in Sydney, about an hour's drive away. Bear was about fourteen and a half years old. The cardiologist did an ultrasound and said, "Whatever you are doing, keep doing it." She said that for her age, she was really good. She had a slight heart murmur but wouldn't need medication yet. Instead, she wanted to check Bear's stomach and do an ultrasound.

We did an ultrasound and biopsy and found that Bear had some liver issues – nodes on the liver. The vet and specialist vet did a biopsy and sent it to pathology. The nodes were not cancerous, so we decided not to operate, especially as one of the nodes was in a non-operable area. We would just monitor her and do another ultrasound and possibly a biopsy further down the track. We also did X-rays, which showed Bear had arthritis in her back, neck and back legs. We started her on monthly arthritis injections and rose-hip vital. It was confirmed Bear was suffering seizures and I had to start her on gabapentin which is a pain and anxiety-relief and seizure medication.

Gabapentin is also a human medication. This seemed to work well for Bear. She only had seizures about once every two to three months. She would always have them in the middle of the night, which made me panic as I wondered what would I do if they were really bad. She had so much medical history, I really only wanted her to be seen by my own vet team.

Anyone who has or had a pet with seizures knows these are frightening. They used to terrify me, but I had to remain as calm as possible for her sake. Needless to say, from the moment Bear was diagnosed with seizures, I never experienced a full night's sleep again. I would wake up (without setting an alarm) twice a night, usually around one to one-thirty a.m. and again around three-thirty or four a.m. I would come out to check on her.

Bear would sleep on the lounge, as she hated sleeping in my room. The vet said she associated her seizures with my room, hence why she wouldn't sleep in there. I would get up and check on her to make sure she didn't have a seizure or was unwell. I used to worry about her so much. I always knew if she'd had a seizure, as she would usually wet herself or poop or sometimes both.

It didn't matter if I came out to check on her. She would wake up, open one eye (like a pirate, LOL) and look at me as if to say, "I am alright, Mum. Don't worry, go back to bed." She would give me a little waggy tail so I knew she was okay. I would kneel down to give her a kiss on her forehead and tell her how much I loved her and to go back to sleep. Then I would cover her up with her blanket, and she would usually give me a kiss straight back on my cheek.

It was almost like Angel had a sixth sense that Bear was either about to have a seizure or had had a seizure. Most times I got up to check on Bear, Angel would lie in her bed, but sometimes Angel would come out to check on Bear with me. Sometimes Bear had had a seizure, and Angel would sit with Bear and look at me with concern. I would reassure them both that everything would be okay. Most times when Bear had a seizure, she would do it in front of me, and Angel would sit aside watching everything unfold, waiting for me to take a deep breath and a sigh of relief. Then she would sit close to Bear and watch her every move.

When Bear stood up and started to wag her tail, Angel would kiss her face and be so excited, as if to say, "You're okay, Bear." They really had a beautiful bond, the two of them, and always comforted each other when the other was sick. They say animals don't know, but they really do. I think animals are very intelligent – more intelligent than some people. They are definitely more intelligent than people give them credit for. Sit with animals quietly and open your heart to them, and they will show you their heart and soul. But, in the meantime, they will help you find your own heart.

At the age of about fifteen-and-a-half, we noticed Bear's arthritis was playing up, so we started to introduce codeine and this seemed to help her. At this age, she was still so very active, running around and playing with Angel. She didn't let anything stop her; she lived life to the fullest. From a very early age, Bear was horrible with taking medication tablets. It didn't matter how you hid them, what you hid them in or crushed them up in. Even if you put them down her throat, she would regurgitate them back up – such a little rascal. We had to get every medication possible to be in liquid form.

Bear also suffered with incontinence for the last nine months of her life, and this was managed without medical intervention. My vet and I discussed this and agreed she was already on enough medication, and if I could manage this without another tablet, to continue to do so. I found Bear's incontinence to be worse at nighttime, or when she was in deep sleeps. If I took Bear out on a regular basis, it was easily managed. I also put puppy pads down in her bed and on her favourite spot on the lounge.

I continued to get up twice a night to check on her for seizures and to wake her up to take her to the toilet. She was so incredibly funny. She had no problem getting up in the middle of the night, as she knew I would change her hot water bottle in the middle of winter, and she would cosy right up to it or the heat packs. (Only the best for Bear.) She would look at me in the middle of winter as if to say, "I will hold on until the morning," and I would say "Come on, Bear, you have to go to the toilet." She would reluctantly go but she always made me go out with her, as if to say, "Well, if I am getting out of a warm bed, so are you." She made me laugh and smile so much. Even as I write this, I am managing to have a little chuckle to myself. I just loved her so much with my heart and soul. She was my world.

Once she was up, I would change her puppy pad to a fresh one. I definitely didn't want her lying in her own urine. I would stand out there with her, and then she would come back in and get back on the lounge and snuggle up. I would change the hot water bottle and wrap it up in her blankets and she would cosy up to it. We would give each other a kiss goodnight, and I would tell her how much I loved her.

She absolutely loved the heat packs on her, especially down her spine and on her back legs. She would move away from it when it got too hot. When the heat packs became cold, she would come over to me while I was watching TV and wag her tail. I would ask her if she wanted to go to the toilet. If there was no response, I would ask if she wanted the heat pack warmed up, and she would kiss me on the cheek and wag her tail as if to say, "That's exactly what I want." She would come out to the kitchen and sit and wait while I warmed up the heat pack in the microwave.

About a year ago, she refused to go to the toilet one night when it was cold and rainy, so I used bribery, as you do. I said, "Bear, if you go to the toilet, I will give you a treat." With that, she was at the back door quicker than I was. I brought her in and she went straight to the kitchen cupboard and sat there as if to say, "Well, I went to the toilet. Now I want my treat." I came in and sat down to watch more TV and noticed she wasn't in the lounge room.

I snuck back in the kitchen, and there she was, staring at the kitchen cupboard. I caved in and gave her the treat. I guess I had to hold up my end of the bargain. Needless to say, from that night on and every night after, when she did her last toilet stop, she would come in and sit at the pantry cupboard waiting for her treat. It became a nightly ritual.

Covid brought about many a hard time for a lot of people. Some people lost their jobs and suffered financial strains, some people lost loved ones and were not able to say their goodbyes or attend funerals. Other people were not able to travel interstate or internationally to see loved ones who became ill. Some people, like me, lived on their own or were elderly and relied on their pets for solace. There was one thing I felt grateful for with Covid: I was able to work from home, and have done so for the past two years. This has enabled me to spend more valuable, precious time with Bear, especially in the days leading up to her passing. The days I would normally travel to work would take me away from home for anywhere between ten and eleven hours per day, five days a week.

In August 2021, Bear got sick, just after my birthday. She was lethargic, drinking a lot of water and wasn't playing. I took her off to her second home (the vet), and they did bloods, and found her pancreas and kidney readings were high. We were concerned she either had pancreatitis or she had kidney disease. The kidney tests were negative for kidney failure, but the vet was leaning towards pancreatitis. Bear had a full weekend of fluids for dehydration, and she seemed to come good, but a couple of days later, she was sick again, so we repeated the bloods and the readings were still high, so we discussed doing an ultrasound.

Bear was booked in for the following Thursday and went back to the vet every day for monitoring and a top up of fluids. She just didn't seem to be getting any better. The vet's saw a slow improvement while she was there, but I couldn't see one. By the Wednesday, the day before the ultrasound appointment, I rang my vet Michelle and vet nurse Crysten, and said, "I think it is Bear's time." She just seemed so unwell, and I didn't want her to suffer. Michelle said I needed to hang in there, as the following day she had the ultrasound, and if we were treating her for the wrong thing, she wasn't going to get better.

I was so scared that Bear had cancer, and to be honest, that's what I was anticipating. I dropped Bear off to the vet on the Thursday morning to have her ultrasound, and came back and logged on to work. I cried my eyes out and could barely compose myself. At lunchtime, the vet nurse Brooke called. Before she could say anything, I was sobbing. But she told me it was okay, and the news was it was treatable and it wasn't cancer. Brooke proceeded to tell me that Rob, the specialist vet who did all the X-rays, CT's and ultrasounds (he had done a few of Bear's previous scans), said there weren't many changes, which he was happy about.

He checked over Bear's liver and there weren't too many changes and her heart didn't seem to be too changed, but they had found that Bear was suffering from colitis, which is similar to IBS (Irritable Bowel Syndrome) and Crohn's, which is what I have. When Brooke started to explain, I told her I knew exactly what it was, as I had Crohn's disease. Brooke relayed this to Vet Specialist Rob and said the two of us couldn't be any more in tune with each other.

Bear was treated with a probiotic for gut health and flaygyl for acute flare of colitis. Within three days, Beary was back to her bossy, vibrant full-of-life self. She was running around crazy and being fussy with food. We were managing Bear's colitis really well, but in the end, it was arthritis that took my little girl from me.

Bear's last days

They say a pet chooses their time to leave us here on earth. They also say we will know when it is their time. We will know or they will tell us. I really struggled with understanding this and kept asking everyone how would I know. Leading up to Bear's passing, two weeks prior I could tell she wasn't herself. She had slowed right down and wasn't playing and running around like she used to. She still had a good appetite but was very picky on what she wanted to eat.

There were some days where I would sit just cuddling Bear and saying, "Is it time, Bear? How do I know if you want to go? How do I know if you have had enough?" I didn't want her to be in pain or suffering, or to have her quality of life diminished. As hard as I knew the decision would be for me to say goodbye, I couldn't keep her alive for my own selfish reasons. Bear and I had sixteen-and-a-half amazing years together. The one last beautiful thing I could do would be to let her go with dignity, as much as I knew it would devastate me.

Sometimes I thought it would be better if she passed away in her sleep. It would be peaceful for her, she would be in her own home environment and the decision to end Bear's life would be taken away from me. It is an extremely tough decision for someone to make, to end their pet's life, but a necessary one and a brave one. Anyone who has made this decision, or needs to make this decision, knows it is one of the hardest decisions to make. I can honestly say it was one of the hardest decisions I have ever had to make over the years, and I have had to make many a hard choice.

On Saturday the 9th of October, I decided to bathe Bear and Angel. Bear used to love her bathtime, but as mentioned previously in the book, she got a bad case of the zoomies. She would zoom around like she was three years old again. As much as I tried to stop her, she ran rings around me like it was a game. This day she must have run around for a good hour and a half, and then finally stopped and had a sleep. Later that night, I could tell she was a bit uncomfortable and obviously suffering from a flare up of arthritis. I warmed up a heat pack for her legs and back.

By the Monday she seemed a bit worse, so I rang the vet's and organised an appointment for the next day and dropped her off. She had some pain relief and they mentioned she had flared her back up. To this day, I regret bathing her that Saturday, and some part of me still says she wouldn't have flared her back up, and she might still be here with me. The rational part of me knows I can't think like this, as if she didn't flare her back up from that, it could have been something else, as her back simply wasn't in a good state.

We decided to try her on a tablet called Antinol which is good for arthritis and can help with other conditions. Alison advised me to give it a try. It was a little on the expensive side, but I thought it was worth a try. I spoke with my vet, and we decided to try it in combination with Bear's monthly arthritis injection. We started her off on two tablets a day, but after a week, we increased it to three a day. I always thought that, like every other time, Bear would overcome this flare up. She had fought so many things, but I knew her age was a factor. I guess we all grow old, and there is never going to be a good time or the right time to say goodbye to our pets. We just never seem to get long enough with them.

This was the downward spiral for Bear. She never seemed to come good, and never did overcome it this time. Over the next four weeks, Bear spent a lot of time in and out of the vet's. She would be there during the day and at home with me at night. She took a lot of pain relief and also IV fluids for dehydration, and my bank account was really starting to suffer. Don't get me wrong, my pets' health and their well-being come before mine. I remember many a time living on rice and noodles and toast just to get by from week to week.

A pet is a lifelong commitment. You don't quit on them when the vet bills start mounting – you find ways to make it work. I have borrowed money off Mum and Dad and even friends at times, to care for Bear. I even worked six days a week in a full-time job, with a part-time job on Saturday nights in a bar, pre-Covid. I did this for five years just to make ends meet. I could see that Bear wasn't herself. She had really flat days when she seemed to be battling exhaustion and she lost a bit of her sparkle and waggy tail.

In the last four weeks of Bear's life, I had tried to brace myself for what was coming. I think deep down in my heart I had a sixth sense that her time with me was coming to an end, but my heart was in denial. I started doing the "what ifs" that I know everyone does. What if I give her some more time? What if when we give her the next arthritis injection, she gets over the line with the use of Antinol?

The what ifs just kept coming, but I knew my vet team and I had done everything. I knew I had given her one of the best, most cherished lives a pet could possibly have. She had a life full of love and happy times – no bad times apart from when she was sick. On Saturday 12th November, a friend came to visit with her daughter. We had been through the darkest of times together and helped each other through almost everything.

On this Saturday, Bear came to life. She ran around with my friend's daughter and played with Angel at tug of war and throwing the ball around. Bear even brought toys to play with, as if to say, "Play with me." My friend commented on how lively Bear was, saying, "I was expecting to see her on death's door the way you had been describing her." By the way Bear was playing, you would think she had just been off-colour. I was in shock actually, and thinking this was the moment she was turning the corner – the moment I had been waiting for.

Angel, Bear and my friend's daughter had been playing for a solid five hours from two p.m. to seven p.m. when we ordered dinner. Bear looked like she'd had a great time, just like her old self, running around play growling. It was like she was going to be okay. My friend's daughter was nine and she was such a little superstar with Bear. She knew Bear hadn't been well and was so kind, giving Bear kisses on the forehead and playing with her and giving her gentle pats. Do we have another possible vet in the making? Let's hope so.

At seven p.m., we all settled in. I fed Bear and Angel a little bit later, as they were only eating one meal a day. Angel had some behavioural problems about a month or so prior to Bear being unwell. She wouldn't eat her dinner unless I sat on the floor with her while she ate. I took Angel to the vet to discuss this, and we gave her some gabapentin in case it was an anxiety issue and tried some different tactics.

Since Bear's passing, Angel is back to normal with her eating, but won't eat in the spot where Bear and her used to eat. Did Angel perhaps know or sense Bear was going to pass and this is why she was acting up with her food? I believe animals and pets communicate with each other. Had Bear told Angel she was going to leave us and this was why Angel was anxious? There was no reason for Angel to suddenly have issues with eating. At first, Bear didn't want to eat her dinner that night, but my friend's daughter sat with her and hand fed her. She talked to Bear until she finally ate. She sat with her the entire time, telling her she was a good girl. Bear loved praise – she was so driven by praise and treats.

The next day, Bear was very quiet. She seemed a bit stiff and sore, but I wasn't surprised with how much running around she did. I took her for a little walk, as the vet said to keep her muscles and legs moving, but only little walks. Bear used to love her walks. She was so excited to see other dogs and people. She was a very social little girl. It didn't matter the size of the dog, she would always go up to every dog on our walks with a little waggy tail.

We were now two days out from her passing, and she wouldn't eat dinner. I tried all her favourite things to get her to eat her dinner. I even drove around to McDonald's to get her chicken nuggets (McDonald's chicken nuggets were her absolutely favourite). When I came home with them, she sniffed them and walked away. I was concerned by this, as when she had been sick in the past, she never turned her nose up at the nuggets.

Monday morning 15th November. Bear still wouldn't eat and I noticed she wasn't drinking as much, so I was really starting to get worried. It was now twenty-four hours since Bear had last eaten, and she seemed weak and uninterested in anything. I was working from home that day and I cried on and off for most of the day. I couldn't believe how lively, full of life and how playful Bear was two days prior. I really felt like Bear was giving up. I had broached my manager weeks previously at work and mentioned to her that if Bear passed away, I would need to take time off work as personal annual leave, as I knew I would be a mess, and the last thing I could think about was work.

During this Monday, the 15th November, I kept saying to Bear, "Is it your time? Are you giving up? How will I know what to do?" I knew what the right thing to do was by her, but I always seemed to be on the merry-go-round of what ifs, and do I make the decision now or later? I had always made Bear a promise and had said to my vet that if Bear's life diminished, I couldn't hold on to her for my selfish sake.

On Tuesday 16th November, I got up at one a.m. to take Bear to the toilet. Normally, she would jump onto the air mattress and walk out to the toilet slowly but unaided. This morning, she stood but sat straight down, as though she had lost feeling in her back legs or couldn't use them. I carried her out to the backyard and put her on the grass. She sat straight down again and stared at me.

As I have mentioned previously in this book, if you are really connected and bonded with your pet, you know them better than anyone. Bear and I were truly connected, heart and soul. I also mentioned previously that Bear and I communicated with our eyes. What happened next shattered me. I felt like I was about to fall in a heap and die. Bear looked at me with the saddest of eyes. If she could have spoken, I know her words to me would have been something like this: "Mum, what are you doing to me? I have had enough of being brave, of the sickness and the medications. It is my time to go. Let me grow my wings. It is my time, let me go now."

With that, I picked her up, gave her the biggest hug and told her that as much as this was going to kill me, I needed to be brave and strong for her. I told her how much I loved her and how good a companion she had been to me. I told her she was the best, and no one could take her place. I thanked her for changing my life and making me a stronger, better, more resilient person, and thanked her for loving me and making me open my life to love again. She showed me kindness and compassion, but also how to laugh and be happy. When she came into my life, I wasn't a happy person. I was broken-down and just existing, but she brought me back to life.

As I write this section of the book, it is Thursday 30th December at ten a.m. I am sitting in the kitchen at the benchtop crying uncontrollably. Angel is in the lounge room but has sensed my upset and has come out to check on me. I think Bear told Angel to look out for me. Many a time I want to cry and go into another room so as to not upset Angel, as I know she is still grieving, but it is like she has a sixth sense and comes looking for me so we can comfort each other.

Once I tucked Bear back into bed, I lay on the floor with her. I told her all about the Rainbow Bridge and explained how there would be other dogs and cats, and also horses like her big brother Sunny, and rabbits and all kinds of animals there to greet her. I told her they would have a pair of wings waiting for her, as they are now guardian angels who will watch over us.

I told her the best part is there is no medication, and no more pain and suffering. I told her she would feel like a pup again. She would be able to run around with the other animals and wouldn't have sore legs or a sore back due to her arthritis. I explained there would be no more scary seizures, and she would be renewed to full health.

I told her the hardest part of being there would be that we wouldn't be physically together anymore, but we would always be connected by our bond and love – our hearts and the beautiful years of memories we created. I said when she missed me, she would be able to feel our love and look down from heaven and see me. I said when I miss her, I would look up at the stars at night and look for the most brightly shining star, knowing it will be her.

At approximately one-forty a.m., I logged on to my work computer and sent an email to the bosses I looked after, and also my manager, and told them I would be taking leave effective immediately, and that I would be off work for the next four days. I sent a separate email to my manager advising her why I was taking my leave – that I needed to make the decision to say goodbye to Bear. I also asked if she could please not tell my co-workers why I had taken leave. I didn't want my co-workers to know the reason I was off in case there was ridicule or talk that it was just a dog. That was the last thing I needed to hear. I will talk about the loss and grief and perceptions in the workplace in the last chapter of my book.

I private messaged my vet and told her that today would be the day I need to say goodbye to Bear. She messaged me a short time later and said, "Oh no, let me get into work, and I will organise something for you." Around ten a.m., the practice manager, Kellie, called to ask if we could do it at five-thirty p.m. My vet was too upset to call me, as she was very bonded with Bear and me. Kellie also asked if it would be okay if a couple of the vet nurses stayed back to support me and also say their goodbyes to Bear, which absolutely touched my heart to know one little girl called Bear had touched so many people's hearts and lives. Whenever Bear was at the vet, she made everyone smile.

Vet nurse Crysten messaged me. It was her day off, but she said she had organised for her mum to look after her son and would be coming along to be there for Bear and me. We truly couldn't have been surrounded by more loving, caring people. The staff there are truly amazing.

I had organised for my friend Mark Kendrigan to take me to the vet, as I knew there was no way I could drive, and I would be scared I wouldn't go through with the decision, even though I knew it was the right one. I spent the entire day with Bear. I hugged her and kissed her and kept reassuring her everything would be okay and that Angel and I would be there every step of the way. I told her Aunty Michelle (vet) and Aunty Crysten (vet nurse) would be there for her, and some of the other vet nurses. I told her it would be just like drifting off to sleep; it would be very peaceful.

Mark turned up at four p.m., and we chatted. I cried and cried, and he gave me the biggest of hugs. While I had spent the day reassuring Bear that she would be okay, I had no one to reassure me I would be okay. I live on my own, and everything is that much harder when you live alone, especially when it comes to matters of the heart. Mark reassured me I would be okay and that he and his wife Julie would be there for me, along with my other friends. He said I was not alone – they would always be there every step of the way.

At five p.m. we got in the car for the last time with Bear. By this time, she was so weak I didn't even need to put her harness on. Anyone who knew Bear well enough knew she had to be in a harness, because if she got out of the car, she would run like the wind, and I would have no hope of getting her back. She was the only dog I knew who could get out of a harness.

We commenced our journey for the last time to the vet for Bear – a place that was like a second home to her, where people loved her just as much as I did. We got to the vet at five-thirty. Teresa, one of the lovely vet receptionists, came out to greet me. She put her arm around me and had tears in her eyes. She took us to the room – a nice area with couches, private from the other practice areas.

Bear's last car ride

The practice manager, Kellie, came in and gave me a hug, and Mark was there the entire time. Then, vet nurses Blake and Lauren came in, and then my vet Michelle . As soon as Michelle and I saw each other, we burst into tears and gave each other a big hug. Michelle had been crying most of the day on and off. Michelle is very bonded with her own dog Molly, the same way Bear and I were, so she could truly understand my level of distress and pain. Vet nurse Crysten came in and gave me the biggest hug. I had asked Crysten if she could assist Michelle; she was touched. Crysten and Michelle had been the most instrumental in Bear's care, so I knew Bear would want them to be there in her final moments.

Angel was very uptight and anxious, running around the euthanasia room a bit pacy and a bit out of sorts. I think she was well aware of what was going on. Vet Michelle gave Bear a sedative first, as she could see Bear was in a bit of pain. By doing this, it made the process easier for Bear. Both Michelle and my friend believe Bear had picked her time to go, and that the reason she ran amok and played so much on the Saturday was to show me the old Bear. They believe it was Bear's way of going out and her last hoorah, as if to say, "Mum, this is how I want you to remember me; not the sick me." I believe, on the Saturday, Bear had chosen her time to go.

I can honestly say the experience was peaceful and relaxed and different to how I had envisaged it. I really didn't know what to expect. I knew going into it my vet, vet nurse and the team there at my local surgery would do everything in their power to make it that way. They truly are remarkable souls, and I feel blessed and grateful that this team are looking after my pets. You hear some real horror stories out there, especially since I joined the grief loss pages. I have heard stories of how the procedure was rushed and there was no empathy, and some people even felt pressured to make the decision.

I knew Bear could not have been in better, more loving arms. Bear was sat next to me with her head on my left leg. When Michelle gave Bear the sedative, I could feel her relax, and then she started snoring. This was confirmed by Michelle. I don't think I had ever heard Bear snore. Angel, on the other hand, at times sounds like a tractor backfiring.

It was at this point, Angel started to calm down and seemed to sense this was time for Bear to leave us. Angel sat on my right side. We talked about some funny memories with Bear, and at no time did I feel rushed. Michelle and Crysten were always right by my side, comforting me and explaining everything. They made this very hard process as comforting as anyone could. I was supported, but more importantly, I knew the love these people had for Bear and me. People who started off as complete strangers now feel like family to me. I care for them immensely and don't see them as my vet team but more like family.

It was time. Michelle asked me if I wanted more time with Bear or if I was ready. In my heart I was never, ever going to be ready, but my head said it is time to let Bear fly high and RIP. I told Michelle I was ready, and with that Mark's, Michelle's and Crysten's and my eyes filled up and Michelle started to administer the euthanasia. Angel dropped her head in my lap and rested it near Bear's. Michelle told me Angel knew Bear was passing away, as per the photos below.

This moment would have made even the strongest, toughest person tear up and cry. There wasn't a dry eye in the room; we were all crying. Let's face it, most marriages and relationships don't last sixteen-and-a-half years these days. The week prior to Bear's passing, I had some questions about the cremation process, as it was always my intention to have Bear cremated and keep her ashes at home with me. I asked Crysten questions, and she advised me to bring Angel with us on the day, as she said if I left Angel at home, she would be looking for Bear.

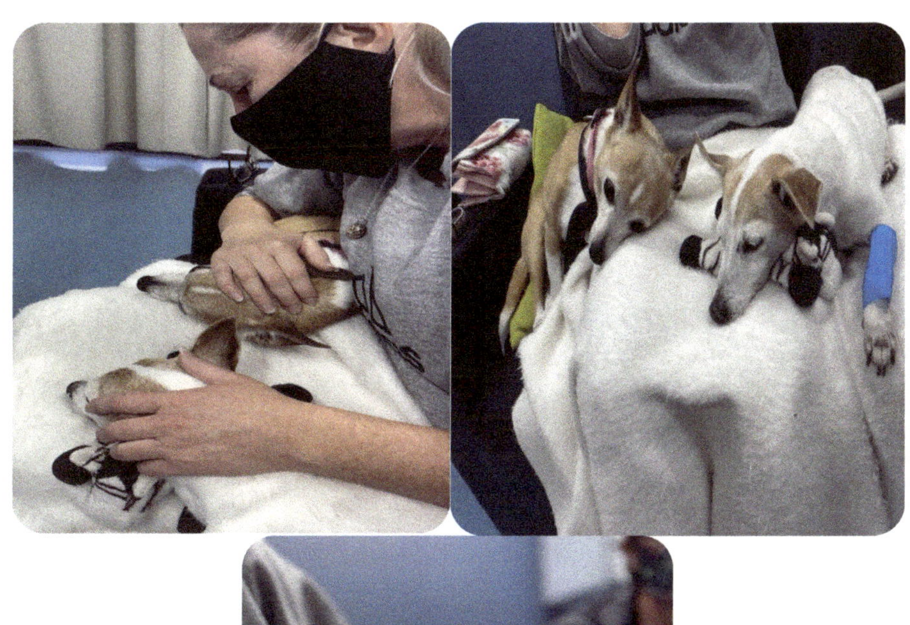

I am glad Angel went with us and that the "Three Musketeers," as I had labelled us, got to be together for that final moment, and so Angel could say her goodbyes as well as me. I knew Angel was one hundred per cent aware of what was going on. She hasn't looked for Bear, but misses her terribly. It has been so hard watching Angel, who is normally full of life and loves playing, become miserable missing her best friend. I know she knew what was happening – we were all so in tune with each other. I only hope one day soon Angel wakes up, and her grieving can ease also.

Once I got Bear's ashes back, I felt like the grieving process had commenced all over again. All the feelings I first felt when I lost Bear all came rushing back. I think, in a funny way, I had almost convinced myself this nightmare wasn't real and Bear was just at the vet, but getting that call to say her ashes had arrived confirmed the nightmare was very real. This was it, there was no turning back, there was no "Can we try that or can we try this medication?" It was real. She was really gone and not coming back, no matter what I did, how much anger I held or how much I cried.

I would like to say, six weeks on, that this process has gotten easier, and I wish I could say for those of you reading this book that this is the case, but it is not. I am still going through the motions. Some days are still harder than others. Christmas has just passed, and this was an extremely tough day. I had to put on a happy face and makeup, as I was going out with friends for lunch. Even though I didn't feel up to it, I know Bear wouldn't want me being at home and crying alone at Christmas.

Traditionally, for the last sixteen years on Christmas morning, Bear took it upon herself to be the official gift unwrapper. She didn't care whether it was hers, Angel's, mine or the neighbours' across the road. As far as she was concerned, if it had wrapping on it, it was hers to go ahead and open. They were always good with the Christmas tree, but I could never put presents under the tree until the night before. She would tear into the presents – it was just so funny to see. Once she had opened presents that weren't hers, and once she realised it wasn't a toy or treat, she would move to the next one.

I remember this one time, on her fifteenth birthday, I had two friends over, and we played pass the parcel. I had wrapped it the night before and put treats on every second wrapper. I have a fifteen-minute video of her playing pass the parcel – this is one of my very precious videos.

The three hardest things about saying goodbye to our fur babies are making the decision; coming out of the surgery with a collar, lead, blanket and the realisation you will never hold your baby again; and lastly, the collecting of the ashes. At this point, the grieving process commences all over again. Anyone who has been through this knows just how hard these moments are.

Bear, as all my fur babies, lived a full and precious life, celebrating birthdays, Christmases and Easter. They receive gifts, just like everyone else. They have such charmed lives full of love and happiness. I have created a beautiful shrine for Bear, which is situated right by the

Bear's Shrine

front door. It is full of her cards, treasures, her ashes and gifts that complete strangers have sent us. Bear loved to sit at the front door watching the world go by. She was such a sticky beak.

Bear and Angel's last Christmas Photo 2021

Bear's fifteenth birthday party

Bear's last birthday – her sweet sixteenth

I was speaking with my friend the other night, and she mentioned she checks her daughter's phone. She told me that when checking it, she came across a conversation between her daughter and her friend talking about Bear, even though my friend's daughter had only met Bear once and it was three days prior to Bear passing away.

It just goes to show the impact our pets make not only on us and our lives, but on others. She still talks about Bear to this day. She mentions to her friends that when she visited Bear, she made her well. I believe this to be true. I believe when my friend and her daughter were here, they bought Bear to life and shared a moment of true happiness and joined in Bear's last hoorah. I will cherish this moment forever, as they helped me to see Bear happy and full of life right before she was really sick. That is the memory I want to hold on to, not one of Bear being sick.

PART 2

Awareness

The special friends Bear left behind (how our pets cope with grief)

Just like us, the pets left behind also grieve. They grieve in the same way, with sadness, misery, not looking forward to playtime, even going off their food and vomiting. When they go off their food, start vomiting and even get diarrhoea, this is known as "fretting." If you feel your pet is fretting, it is best to get a vet to check over your pet. I know Angel is missing Bear. She isn't fretting, but is really sad and not wanting to play all of her favourite games. It is like she has lost interest in all the things she loves. Most days, she just lays in her bed whining.

Also, with our pets there is no time limit for how long they will grieve for their friend. It really is at the individual pet's pace. I keep in mind Bear and Angel were left on their own for five days a week for long days, ten to twelve hours. They only had each other during this time, so their bond was particularly strong. Bear's best friend was Angel. Angel is a mini foxy-Chihuahua who entered Bear's life when Bear was about five years old. At the time, my ex-fiancé and I decided, with us both working full time, it might be nice to have a friend for Bear to keep her company.

Angel was around ten weeks old when we got her from a pet store. At first, Bear sniffed her and didn't seem to want much to do with her. We made such a fuss over Angel, as she was so little, and she was and still is to this day very needy. Bear was always so independent. She would play in the garden, chase birds, butterflies and lizards and would play with her toys. After a week and a half of Bear rejecting Angel and not wanting anything to do with her, we started to worry about the decision we had made in getting a companion for Bear. We took both Bear and Angel to the vet.

The vet asked us to run him through a typical day. We explained that we were fussing more over Angel, as she was so little and a pup, and explained that when we got home from work, we would pick Angel up first and give her the first kiss and cuddle. We thought we were doing the right thing, as she was the pup. The vet corrected us straightaway and said we were doing all the wrong things. He said we needed to pat Bear first, give Bear the first of the attention, feed Bear first, play with Bear first and give treats to Bear first. He explained that Bear was the first dog in the family, and that she is the alpha and always needs to come first. The pup wouldn't realise anything different, as she was new to the environment.

Once we changed the routine back to Bear being first at everything (LOL, even bath time), within a week, Bear and Angel became the absolute best of friends. They would play for hours together, chasing each other through the house. I am sure they even played hide-and-seek, because Bear would go into one of the rooms and jump up on the bed, and Angel would come out, frantic, as if to say, "I can't find Bear."

Watching them play and love each other was so precious and beautiful. They had the most wonderful bond. They never ever fought, not once, not even over food. They sometimes got in the same bed together if one was sick, to provide comfort. Bear was like a little mother to Angel. She toilet trained her for us, and was the one who taught Angel how to fit in with our lifestyle.

Angel on the left, Bear on the right

We also have a cat named Mr. Puss. Puss weighs 9.4 kg – he's much bigger than the two little ladies, Angel and Bear. Puss was always trying to be the alpha pet in the home, but there was no way Bear was having any of that. Mr. Puss would boss Angel around – he knew Angel was scared of him. Sometimes, Puss would back Angel into a corner and full-on bully her, swiping at her and boxing her. Bear would rush in and challenge Puss. She would sit in front of Puss, puff her chest up to make herself look bigger, and sit there glaring at him. Puss would often try to box Bear, but Bear would just sit there looking at him as if to say, "Is that the best you can do?"

Bear got on with any animal, child or person. She really did have the sweetest, calmest and most vibrant personality I have ever seen in a dog. Angel is eleven years old this Christmas, and she is completely devastated by the loss of her best friend. As I write this chapter, we are approaching four weeks since we said goodbye to Bear, and she is still the same. She lies in her bed all day, staring into space. She won't play with the ball or play tug-of-war, two of her very favourite games she would play with me when Bear had had enough of playtime.

Angel is grieving the loss of Bear as much as I am, and it honestly breaks my heart that she feels so lost and sad. At times, it looks like she has been crying, as she has the runny eye marks down her face. Some nights, after dinner, she walks around with a stuffed toy in her mouth, whimpering. It's almost as if to say, "Where is Bear? When is she coming home? I miss her." It doesn't seem to matter how many kisses or hugs I give, or how much I try to play with her, as it doesn't lift her mood.

The week after Bear left us for the Rainbow Bridge, the vet's wanted to keep an eye on Angel to make sure she didn't fret, as that was their concern as well as mine. They did a check-up on her, and her weight was good, along with her heart murmur. They did a full check-up, asked questions and explained that our pets go through a grieving period as much as we do. My vet said I should keep an eye on her and make sure she kept eating and didn't have diarrhoea or vomiting, and that just like us, it will take time for her to come around.

I honestly believe Angel knows Bear has left us for the Rainbow Bridge, but like me, I think she desperately wants Bear to be here. As hard as it is for me to watch Angel grieve, it is also beautiful, as now each morning and night, she likes to lick Bear's urn, which we say good morning and good night to. I know Angel understands, and I think that is why she is so sad, because she knows Bear isn't coming back.

The vet suggested I keep the routine the same as I had when Bear was still with us. She said changing anything could make the grieving process harder for her. I have kept breakfast and dinner time the same, Bear's bowl is still in the same place. I have kept the foods the same. Treat time is still the same time, around twelve p.m. The only things I have introduced to the routine is to allow Angel to sleep with me, as this provides comfort to the both of us, and a daily walk.

Even though Angel has a heart murmur, the vet suggested a walk in the fresh air and sunshine would do us both the world of good. I have found this has slightly lifted her mood. She is very alert on our walks, smelling and looking around at everything, and at times has a waggy tail. She is more approachable with other dogs. When we used to walk with Bear, Angel would show aggression to other people and dogs who came near us. I'm not sure if this was just Angel being protective.

Pets grieve the same way we do. Prior to the pandemic, I would work full time five days a week. I would be gone, Monday to Friday, for approximately ten to twelve hours per day. They kept each other comforted, protected each other and had someone to play with, and now all of a sudden, I feel like Angel is lost without Bear and doesn't know what to do. I think Angel would love the companionship of another dog, but I am not ready to open my heart. In a way, I would feel like I was betraying Bear and replacing her, and even though I know deep in my heart that's not what I would be doing, and I know Bear would love another dog to experience the wonderful loving life she had, I know I am not ready.

I have noticed, since Bear left us, Angel has one behavioural trait which has dramatically changed. Angel has always been a very nervous dog, even as a pup outside of her home environment. If other dogs or people came near us, she would be very snappy and snarly. When I walked her and Bear together, when people or other dogs walked towards us, she would be completely off her tree, barking and snarling. Now it is just her and I walking, I have noticed she doesn't react like this anymore. Even the other day, my neighbour's toy poodle came up to her and sniffed her. She seemed uncertain, but there was no barking and snarling. I am not sure if Angel used to do this thinking that she needed to protect Bear, but she is now a lot better on our walks.

Everyone is different, and as I have mentioned previously in my chapter about grief, there are no rights and wrongs, and there are no time limits. Some people go out and get another pet more or less straightaway and have found that comforting and that it helps them move forward, and that's okay. I know of people like me who have been so grief-stricken, they weren't able to get another pet for many years – anywhere between two and six years.

In a way, I am lucky. I still have four other pets who need me, which I think helps with my grief. They are still relying on me to feed them, provide love and care for them. I can honestly say, if I had no other pets and lost Bear, I think I would need to get another dog, not to fill the void, but to love and care for another pet and feel that level of comfort and support that pets provide.

Mr. Puss entered our lives while I was living in the remote country town with my ex-fiancé. He was a stray feral kitten around seven weeks old. He was one of three. In the town I lived in, there was an issue with stray animals – it was very sad to see. We were flooded in by flood waters from Queensland, and the SES had come to town to assist with the floods. They also had to build a levy bank around the town. They mentioned there were three feral kittens and asked around if anyone wanted them. My ex-fiancé and I always wanted to get a couple of cats when we moved to Mudgee, where we had purchased twenty-five acres, as we were going to have a barn and stables.

I, being the animal lover I am, was worried about what was going to happen to the three feral kittens, so my ex and I discussed getting one of them, and we chose the black one. Of course, he happened to be the feistiest of all three. I knew both Angel and Bear would be fine with the introduction of a new pet, as I had had a bird previously – a rainbow lorikeet – named Tiger. Bear used to love Tiger, and Tiger would ride around on Bear's back. Tiger passed away about five years ago.

SES rang us that afternoon to say they had captured the little black kitten but to be extremely careful, as he had torn three SES guys' hands to shreds. They said he was so feral, did we really think we wanted him? I knew we could change him in time. We picked him up and brought him home, and set him up in the bathroom. He was tiny. This kitten had a lot of fleas. To be precise, he was full of fleas, so we bathed him. That was interesting, to say the least. When we were drying him, we could see what we thought was blood, so we checked him for cuts and sores but couldn't see any, so I took a photo of the towel to show the vet.

A town folk gave us some flea powder. Once the kitten was bathed and dried, my ex doused it in flea powder, and he went from being black to white. That night, my ex read up on this flea powder and said, "Oh no." I asked what was wrong, and he said, "This stuff was banned a few years ago, as it is toxic and has killed pets." I was so fearful that in the morning we would wake up and have a dead kitten. To our surprise, we woke up and the kitten was awake, all bright-eyed, and the towel was covered in dead fleas. We never saw another flea on him again.

As we were in a remote location, the vet only came to town twice a week, so we booked an appointment with the vet. She weighed him and said he only weighed 740 grams. No wonder, he was tiny, and when I showed her the photo, she said that it wasn't blood, and that was flea faeces. She said, given approximately another week, he would have been dead. She said he was so emaciated with the fleas, and malnourished.

Puss's first night at home with us. What fleas?

He would hiss and swipe every time we went near him. It took us about six weeks to be able to pat him, and a further two weeks on from that, we started to gradually open the bathroom door little by little so Bear, Angel and Puss could start the slow process of learning to live with each other. Who would have thought that kitten weighing 740 grams would turn out to be a 9.4 kg black panther now?

Puss has never been a smoocher. He won't sit on your lap, he won't let you pick him up and he is very skittish if someone new comes to the house. Over time, he gets to know different people's smell and voice, but at first, he will run and hide. He will come up for pats and belly rubs and lets me scratch his back and give him kisses. Over the years, he has gotten so much better. I think though, when they are feral, they are so used to fighting or fleeing that that instinct always remains with them. Any changes to the household, and he just doesn't cope well.

Puss and Bear always clashed. Puss wanted top spot on the hierarchy ladder, and Bear was just never going to relinquish it. Over the many years, they had learned to co-exist together, but were never what I would call friends. Sometimes, Puss would take sly swipes at Bear if I wasn't watching, but most of the time it was harmonious.

Now that Bear is no longer with us, I have seen some big changes in Puss. I know Puss is aware that Bear is no longer with us. At first, especially the first two to three days, I could see him going in and out of the rooms, and he would look at me strangely, as much as to say, "Bear is missing." I kept telling Puss that Miss Beary went to the Rainbow Bridge. The first week I could tell Puss was a bit out of sorts. Would I say Puss misses Bear? I don't believe so; I believe he has taken the top spot, as Angel just doesn't seem fussed whether she is boss lady or not.

As mentioned before, Puss is not a smoochy sort of a cat. However, since Bear has passed, he has started to sit under my work desk when I work from home due to Covid, curled up next to my feet as if to say, "I am here, Mum." At nighttime, he lies on the lounge where Bear used to lie, and although I don't believe Puss is grieving, I feel he is trying to reach out to me and offer me comfort while I am grieving.

He now has started to rest his head on my lap, and he reaches out his front paw and rests it on my leg. When he is lying on the lounge and I am crying, he seems to know, and while crying, he starts to knead with that one paw as if to say, "It's okay, Mum." He also follows me around the house more looking for me. Another thing I have noticed is he has stopped bullying Angel, and they seem a bit more relaxed around each other, which is lovely to see.

They say animals don't know and are not intelligent, but they are. They also say cats are hard to train, which is not true. Puss knows lots of words and phrases and is very obedient. He will sit, come when I call him and he knows lots of words like "birdies", "tuna" and "bedtime", "Where's Angel?" He also knows the words "hungry" and "mince" – he really is a funny fellow.

Nala the rabbit and Bear were very special friends. They say you can't have a rabbit with dogs, particularly a Jack Russell. Most people know Jack Russells are hunting dogs and bred to hunt rabbits. Bear and Nala use to run around the backyard together. Bear would run around near her, but you could see she was watching not to get too close. Of a nighttime when I used to bring Nala out to sit on my lap, Bear would get on the lounge with us and groom Nala, cleaning her back, neck and licking the insides of her ears.

Nala use to go to sleep whilst Bear was doing this – she loved it. In fact, when Bear stopped, Nala would look around to see why it stopped. The only thing Nala didn't like was when Bear licked her eyes. I have videos of Bear doing this and have videos of them playing out in the backyard together. People could not believe what they were seeing. I would often say to Bear, "I don't know if you love Nala or you secretly want to eat her, LOL."

Bear and Angel have never shown Nala any aggression or gone to her cage. One of my vets said the reason all these unlikely pets got on so well is due to the amount of love I have for them and the way I have introduced them and interacted with them. I don't think Nala is grieving, but I know she would be missing her grooming sessions, as

Who said a rabbit and a dog can't be besties?

I certainly am not going to lick her, LOL. See, when you look back on nice memories or funny memories of your pets, you will smile. I can't say I have started to laugh yet, but I have found myself smiling at times, especially writing this book about Bear and looking at all the beautiful photos I have.

Sunny the horse is Bear's big brother – he is a palomino. Although Sunny doesn't live with us because he is on agistment, I have some very fond moments of the two of them. When I lived in the remote location with my ex-fiancé, there were about six horses roaming the countryside. As a little girl, I did horse riding, but ended up chucking a tanty when Mum and Dad would not buy me a horse, so I stopped horse riding. I always loved palominos. It was always a dream of mine to get a horse one day. (Now I know why Mum and Dad wouldn't buy me one all those years ago – they cost an arm and a leg. They really do eat you out of home and house.)

While out in this location one day, I was bored and decided to go and take carrots out to the horses. Sunny came straight up to me, no hesitation. I bonded with him immediately. The ex was very hesitant, as he didn't trust the horse, but I did. Animals can sense if you have a fear and sense what sort of person you are. After about a year, we found out who owned my horse and purchased him for five hundred dollars. It was one of the happiest days of my life.

It wasn't long before Sunny worked out where we lived in town. Another smart animal, he would come to the house where we lived and would kick the Colorbond fence on the side where our bedroom was. This would be mostly around twelve o'clock at night. Out I would go with some hay and food and hang over the fence feeding him.

During the day, when Sunny would come to the house to visit, I would take Bear out and hold her over the fence, and she would lick Sunny's face madly. It was such a precious sight to watch, and I could see Sunny looking at me as if to ask what the hell the dog was doing to him, but he would just stand there and take it all in. Bear loved the smell of Sunny. She used to get so excited when she saw him. He was just another friend to her, but on a bigger scale. I could picture the two of them running around together on acreage.

Two years later, my ex and I split, and sadly I had to move back home and unfortunately part with Sunny. I gave him away to a lady who was an equine vet nurse and I always kept in contact with her for updates. I was completely devastated losing Sunny, but fast-forward six years and the universe had the most reuniting story, as we were brought back together and now he gets to live out the remainder of his life with me.

While living in the country, I got to do so many amazing things. One day, we were given a joey kangaroo whose mother had been hit by a car. Where we lived was so remote, there were no wires carers nearby. We spoke to one and made arrangements what to do with the joey and how to care for it. Apparently, the mother kangaroo pouches are extremely insulated, so we needed to make sure we offered the same warmth to the joey, and as it was the middle of winter, this meant sleeping the joey in bed with the electric blanket on with a blanket inside a pillow case.

We also obtained some Di-Vetelact to feed the joey. We had the joey for a few days until we managed to get him to a wires career. Below are a couple of pictures of Bear and Angel with the joey. Bear, in her stride, went straight up to the joey, smelt it, and wagged her tail as if to say, "Welcome, let's play."

Angel less certain of this new addition

How our pets want us to remember them (signs they send us)

I believe our pets would want us to cherish their memories, remember the good times and most of all, I believe they would want us to keep moving forward. I know Bear wouldn't want me to stay sad for too long. She brought so much love and happiness into my life, and she would want me to hold on to that tightly to keep moving forward.

Bear had a way of making you feel like no matter what was happening, things would somehow work out. She would be looking down on me and saying, "Mum, don't cry. Remember how much I made you laugh. Remember the crazy zoomies I used to do. I have given you so many tools to use for the rest of your life – now use those tools."

I believe our pets wouldn't want us to stay in grief mode. Each and every one of them had a purpose. They would want us to look at their pictures and videos with love in our hearts, a smile and to talk about them. They would want us to keep their memory alive in our hearts, and they would want us to tell their funny stories with a smile on our face.

They say if we are open to it, our pets will show us signs as a way of confirming they are still around us and with us spiritually. It is also said that if you ask them to, they will show signs sometimes in the most weird but wonderful of ways. I have heard so many different stories from other pet parents of the signs they have been shown, and it truly makes my heart melt.

I have heard of stories where a pelican has appeared in a lake near a pet parent's house, where there had never been a pelican in the lake prior to the pet passing over. I have heard of blue wrens landing on someone's patio while they were sitting having a coffee, and landing quite close to the person. We all know wild birds don't come too close, and blue wrens are also very hard to find.

They say the most common signs that a pet has crossed over are feathers landing at your feet, floating down in front of you, landing on your car or suddenly appearing out of nowhere; coins; smells; butterflies and dragonflies. Dragonflies are meant to be a powerful sign. They also say that pets communicate by playing silly buggers with your electricals, making lights flicker and light bulbs blow, even televisions pixelating.

Spiritual meanings of signs our pets send to us:

Credit: Feathers - Reference to Amanda APS and Bill Tabone APS (The Spiritual Meaning Of Feathers | by Amanda APS and Bill Tabone APS | Medium)

Feathers. Have you ever found a feather and wondered if this was a sign from a passed loved one? Or maybe it's a sign of a higher power watching over me, guiding me? Is it a sign from Angels? Sometimes when I miss a loved one on the other side, I'll ask for them to show me a sign by giving me a feather. Sometimes if life is treating me rough, I'll ask for a sign. We all need a little reminder we are loved and thought of. When an Angel or our loved ones in the afterlife send you a feather, always be mindful of the colour, as they're trying to tell you something so you need to pay attention. White also means purification, hope and faith. The higher realms are looking out for you. It's also a message from your loved ones on the other side letting you know they're okay.

Credit Reference to Butterflies – Your tango by Maatie Kalokoh. Written on Aug 23, 2021

White Butterfly Meaning: Purity, spiritual transformation, communication from deceased loved ones, good luck and peace.

Credit Reference to Coins by Erica Hernandez Spiritual Meanings: Finding Coins – Erica L Hernandez

Finding coins on the ground or in any other unusual place brings to mind the saying: "pennies from heaven." Spirits, guardian angels, guides, whatever you call them, they keep an eye on us, figuratively speaking. They're there with us all the time and when we open our hearts to them, we begin to notice how they communicate. They let us know when we're on the right path for our soul by leaving us little signs, which might be in the form of coins.

When we are on the right path, they leave signs in the material world for us to find. Your guides may drop pennies in your path, leave you feathers, or pretty or heart-shaped stones. They direct you to see repeating numbers. They leave you signs you find suddenly, and only you will know the significance of them. If they're young spirits, they may play silly pranks on you. They're letting you know that they're there, with you, watching over you, letting you know when you're on the right path. It may be something you are thinking or something you are doing that is "right" for your soul path. They want you to know that you're on the right path, so they leave you a sign.

As I continue with this chapter, I am now in week three since losing Bear. I say good night and good morning to Bear and talk to her as though she is here. I know in my heart she can hear me. I have asked her to show me signs and have received the following:

- A few days after Bear passed over, I talked to my boss, who was very compassionate about my loss. She would ring me every day to make sure I was okay. I told her I could smell hot apple pie in my house like it was baking in my oven. My boss said, "You didn't leave something in the oven, did you?" I told my boss I hadn't cooked any food since Bear passed. She told me to go out the front and back to see if one of my neighbours was cooking it. I did that and definitely no hot apple pie smells outside. I came back in and stood near my kitchen and could smell it again. Ten minutes later the smell was gone. One of my friends, who is spiritual, told me to think bigger. She said, "What do you think of when you smell fresh hot apple pie baking?" I said, "I feel like it's sweet." She said, "No, it's like comfort food, like being at home." She felt it was Nana reaching out to let me know Bear was with her and safe – a way of comforting me.
- Sunday 28th November. I have a police dog stuffed toy which sits on my bedside table. It had been there for two years and never moved apart from when I dusted. I came in to get ready for bed and it was on the floor. There was no way it could have gotten there.
- Monday 29th November. A grey feather landed at my feet. It was extremely soft and gently moving in the slight breeze. There was not a single bird to be seen.
- Tuesday 30th November. I saw a dragonfly right outside my office window. I have lived in the same house for almost eight years and honestly can't recall ever seeing a dragonfly in my backyard. Many a time I wondered if they even still existed. On this day, I happened to look at the window and saw it. I went out into the backyard and watched it and it was zooming around really quickly. It reminded me of when Bear used to

get excited and wound up, and she would end up zooming around everywhere. I watched this dragonfly in awe for about five minutes, then as I sat down at my desk, I looked back out the same window and saw a baby dragonfly.

- Monday 6th December. I was half an hour away from home, visiting my horse. I went to shut my boot after putting some food in there and noticed a ladybug on the spoiler of the car. I didn't think much of it but drove home and the ladybug was in the exact same spot on my spoiler, even though at times I drove at 90 kilometres per hour.
- Wednesday 8th December. Once again, I went to get ready for bed and the police dog toy was on the floor in the exact same spot as the other night. This occurred again on the night of Tuesday 21st December.

Where the Police dog is normally *Police dog on the floor*

- On numerous occasions, I have had multiple electrical signs. My iPod that I use when I go to the gym is switched off each time I finish my gym session. However, a few times around one-thirty and three-thirty a.m., I have been able to hear very faint music. When I start walking around my room, the closer I got to my gym bag, I could hear my iPod was playing. Funnily enough, it was around these times every morning that I would get up and check on Bear to make sure she hadn't had a seizure.

- I keep my iPad turned off and only use it on the odd occasion. However, some mornings at around seven-thirty to eight-thirty, my iPad alarm would sound. I have no alarms set on my iPad, and these are the times that normally Bear and Angel would be fed their breakfast.

- Sunday 27th February. At nine a.m., I was brushing my teeth thinking about Bear and this book I have written. I finished brushing my teeth and put my electric toothbrush back on its dock and proceeded to do my makeup. As I was doing my makeup, I thought about this journey, and just then my electric toothbrush turned on and I struggled to turn it off at the button. It was at this moment I had tears well up as I knew this was Bear reaching out, saying to me, "Mum, you're awesome. You are going to help so many people. Keep going, I know you can do it."

Don't be afraid to ask your pets to send you signs that they are still around. When I started asking Bear to please start sending me signs, I was being shown signs. This can offer a great deal of support and comfort, and has confirmed for me that even though I can't see her or touch her, she is in fact still around me. The signs they send will be true confirmation that it is in fact them behind the signs.

What do we do when our loved one passes away?

Many people have asked me this question. Do you cremate your pet or bury them, and how do you honour them? This is something that only you will know. It was always my decision to have my pets cremated when that time came. When you bury a pet, you need to keep in mind if that will be your forever home. What happens if you move house? By cremating Bear, I can place her in her favourite spot in front of the door. If I move house, she will be able to come with me. I always want my pets to be with me, whether they are here or if they have crossed over the Rainbow Bridge.

I have spoken to other people who have cremated their pet and scattered their ashes in the pet's favourite places, such as the beach or a park. How do you honour your pet? There are many ways to do this. For me, to honour Bear, it was writing this book. Bear would want me to advocate and help others. She would want me to bring about awareness about grief, but more importantly, she would want me to keep her memory alive by remembering her and talking about her. I also plan to get a tattoo. I have a few different drawings which have been made up and when I reach the right one, I will know and I will then organise to have the tattoo placed on my shoulder. I also wear a piece of jewellery with her fur inside.

There are so many things you can do, from tattoos, jewellery, having canvases made, paintings, even teddy bears with some of your pet's ashes placed within the teddy bear. People have had special memorial plaques designed, while others have planted plants such as a rose garden with an angel or a plaque next to the rose tree, cushions and even blankets are another nice memorial piece. There are so many different ways. Choose the one which will provide you with the most comfort. For me, having a tattoo of Bear's paw print along with the necklace with her fur brings me a level of comfort, almost like she is with me everywhere I go.

Regardless of what you decide to do, the most important thing to remember is you have the memories deep inside your heart. These will never fade – they will always be with you every second of the day. They will never be lost, nor will you have to worry about what happens when you move house.

Kind acts from strangers

I am truly amazed at the kindness of complete strangers. In fact, complete strangers have been better than some of my friends who I thought would be there for me but haven't even reached out. It is true what they say – you discover who your true friends are in your darkest and deepest hour.

Three weeks on and I have received flowers, cards, gift boxes, a pillow with Bear's picture and even more recently, yesterday a beautiful rainbow bracelet from a lady in the Jack Russell Group I have been a part of for many years. I have never met this lady, and in fact she lives in a different state, but she sent me the bracelet with a beautiful card and some beautiful words. It goes to show you just how many people have walked in our shoes; they have been here and have survived the painful journey. Their words are not only comforting but provided me with hope and encouragement that I will get through this, just as I hope you do too.

On Monday 6th December, I was driving home from seeing my horse when I saw a man walking a Jack Russell that looked a lot like Bear. As you can imagine, I burst into tears, sobbing and almost feeling like I was having a panic attack. I felt like I couldn't catch my breath or see the road. I made the wise decision to pull over and gain composure (if that was even possible). I pulled off the main road down a side street and parked in front of houses.

As I was crying, I noticed an older lady come to collect her bin near to where I had parked. She must have noticed I was not in a good state. She approached my car and asked if I was okay. I thanked her and said I would be. She said, "Lovey, you look like you're in such a state. Is there anything I can do for you, or someone I can call?" I told her no and that I just needed to sit there for a couple of minutes until I calmed down. She said okay, but if I needed anything to knock on her door, and to look after myself. I thanked her very much for her concern. Needless to say, that touched my heart. I went to the shops a couple of days later, bought her a box of chocolates and a thank you card and left them on her doorstep.

After I lost Bear, my friend, a counsellor, suggested I join some pet loss support groups. I joined two of them and was blown away with how many people all over the world are feeling exactly the same way I am. When I posted, some of them even reached out to me personally through instant messenger and offered words of comfort and support.

I think it is really important for everyone going through this process to remember you are definitely not alone. There are many people out there who care and have been through this. All you need to do is reach out, keep communicating and more importantly, do not shut yourself off from others. Please don't ever think you are alone or have to face this journey on your own.

Bear's vet team

I have no idea where to start with this chapter but to say what an amazing team of people I have looking after my pets. The staff at my local vet have not only been amazing with their knowledge and care, but showed Bear and I so much kindness and humility. Kindness, and going above and beyond, in this day and age is unheard of, and to find a team in the one place under the one roof … Boy, did I get lucky. I used to go to a previous vet where I was treated like a number and not a person; I was part of a money-making production line. My pets were not treated as important, and everything was about the money. At every opportunity, this vet practice upsold me products such as foods and medications.

I wrote a letter to my local vet's head office summarising exactly how great my team was:

"I write this letter in way of compliment and gratitude to the staff at my local vet. I have been attending this practice for a few years with all four of my pets (two dogs, a cat and a rabbit). My regular vets are Erin Short and Michelle Okron. I can't highly praise the staff at this practice enough. They are compassionate, always go above and beyond and show complete care and support, not only for my pets but for me too.

One of my dogs, Bear, a sixteen-year-old Jack Russell, has numerous health problems ranging from liver issues to heart murmur, arthritis and seizures. There has been many a time I have needed to rush her in there to be seen, either for seizures or the arthritis in her back and legs. They always fit me in, and go out of their way to be kind and comforting and support not just Bear but myself. I believe to this day, I am so lucky to still have Bear and feel a lot of this is due to their care, expertise and knowledge.

Just this past two weeks, Bear became ill. Dr. Michelle investigated her thoroughly, from blood tests to urine tests, and organised for Bear to have an ultrasound, as her bloods were showing high kidney and pancreas readings. She was placed on a drip over the weekend, as she was showing dehydration. This was all done in an extremely timely manner. The following week, she was booked in for an ultrasound, and during that week Bear started to get sicker. I dropped her in every day for three days to have pain relief and fluids. Last Tuesday evening, Bear seemed to be at a point where I didn't think she was going to overcome what was going on. During those three days, Dr. Erin and Dr. Sandy took care of Bear, as Michelle was away. Erin and Sandy constantly kept me up to date with what was happening and the plan of attack. They always explained things and comforted me. I have a stress-related condition called Crohn's and could feel myself starting with a flare. The level of comfort and support that Erin and Sandy provided was a godsend and I can't thank them enough. The vets and vet nurses could see that Bear was making an improvement. However, Bear didn't seem like she was improving when she was at home.

I was almost ready to call it a day for Bear, as she has been such an amazing little companion. I was truly scared I was going to lose her and that it was quite possibly something as serious as cancer. Both Crysten and Michelle reached out to me. They were extremely caring and kind and advised me we were only a day away from getting Bear's ultrasound and to not give up on her, as this could be something that could be managed and treated.

Dr. Rob completed Bear's ultrasound and it turns out she has colitis – a treatable and manageable condition. I feel awful when I think that I could have possibly given up on Bear. I am forever grateful for Crysten and Michelle reaching out to me, as I still have her with me and get to spend more valuable time with her. For me, my pets are not pets, they are like my children. Everyone knows how much they mean to me and treat my pets accordingly. I don't trust many people with my pets, but I can say wholeheartedly I trust every staff member there with their lives.

Prior to being at my local vet, I attended another local practice for about eleven years. While at this practice, I was treated like a number in a production line. I was sold and upsold products all the time and I honestly believe if I was still attending that practice that I would not have Bear with me today.

That other practice does not have the animals' care or health at heart, they care more about the money and the number of people they can get in and out of the door. My local vet team are the opposite: they have every pet at heart. This is the motto I love and this is the motto I am more than happy to spend my money on.

I honestly needed to write this letter by way of recognising everyone there. They are certainly amazing, each and every one of them, and they deserve to be recognised. The practice is extremely busy, but they manage to make everyone feel like they are number one and important. At this practice, I am not treated as part of a money-making production line, but as an important person with important pets. It doesn't matter how many questions I have, I am always given the time to have all my questions answered. I am offered reassurance and followed up by calls from the vet nurses.

This practice is one of the best within NSW. Kelly is not only an effective practice manager, she still takes time to get to know the pets and their mums and dads. Kelly is always professional in her dealings and at times has provided me with support and comfort when Bear has been sick. Most practice managers you don't even see, let alone get to know.

Every single staff member is paramount in the success of this practice, but I do need to make a special mention of the following staff, mainly due to the level of interaction with my pets. I would also like to point out I don't know any of the staff on a personal level, just from attending the practice with my pets.

Vets – Erin, Sandy and Michelle have been amazing. All three have such great knowledge and passion for what they do. They love the pets and take the time to make sure you understand what is happening with your pet. At no point have I ever felt like they were being vague or not knowledgeable. They always have my pets' best interest at heart, and whenever I have questions, they are always able to answer them in a concise and understandable way. I am extremely grateful to them. I can't recommend or thank them enough.

Vet nurses – Lauren, Brooke, Jen and Blake. They have had so many dealings with Bear, and once again their knowledge, care and passion needs to be highlighted and recognised. Whenever I have had Bear in there, they have always rung and updated me. I feel I can always ring them if I have a trivial question, and if they can't answer it, they always follow up with the vet and always get back to me.

Bear is very at ease going to any of them in the practice, and for this reason, I know when I leave her, she is in the very best hands. In fact, I don't know too many dogs that enjoy going to the vet, but for some reason, Bear enjoys seeing everyone there. I can tell she feels at ease and comfortable. (I need to be honest, she has spent a lot of time there, especially over this past year.) I always see them giving her cuddles and attention, so for me, knowing I can leave her with them and know she is being loved and cared for is the biggest ease off my shoulders.

Reception – Theresa, Angela and Bec. For very much the same reasons as above. When they answer the phone, they always have the same happy, helpful disposition. They have gotten to know me and my pets and always take an interest in how they all are, how I am and how my day has been. The level of customer service at this practice is second to none.

Out of everyone, I need to make a very special mention to Crysten and Dr. Michelle. They are both extremely valuable to this practice. I think, out of everyone at the practice, Michelle and Crysten have had the most to do with my pets, especially Bear. At times when I have been so worried about Bear, they have reached out to me with phone calls to see how Bear is doing but to also see how I am. They have comforted me and provided such kindness. I have never known people who start out as complete strangers but have so much care and compassion. Due to Michelle's interest and care in Bear, I would like to say thank you. She is a big part of the reason I still have time left with Bear in her old age, and for this I could not be more grateful.

Also, in the past two weeks, Crysten has messaged me in her own time, just checking in on Bear and getting regular updates to see how she was doing. This just goes to show the level of care and commitment she has, and what a special person Crysten is. She has a love and genuine passion for the care she provides to the pets she comes in contact with. It is even funny at home, as Bear has gotten to know Crysten and Michelle's names. Bear has a very big vocabulary of words, and when I mention their names, she either runs to the door as if to say, "Are we going in the car?" or she runs to get her lead. When she sees Michelle and Crysten, her tail wags so much. I can see the love my Bear has for Michelle and Crysten.

The level of service this practice provides is like nothing I have come across of late. Hardly any businesses have this level of professionalism, care, kindness or such high standards. I don't sit and take the time out to write letters like this. For me to write a letter like this, I really have to be impressed. I am often recommending my vet team to all my friends and family and even strangers. I found myself at a store the other day, and I struck up a conversation about pets with the checkout operator and told her all about my vet team.

I hope this letter finds the right person in head office, and I hope you are able to reach out to the team and acknowledge and commend them for the great and hard work they are doing. I feel so privileged that I am able to say my pets could not be in any better care. I feel like I found the best team and feel like they are just like extended family members now.

Recognition of our Vets

The pandemic has changed the way our vets work and the stresses that come with the job, and I believe they have a really hard job. They are either comforting someone who is saying goodbye to a beloved pet, telling someone bad news that their pet has something serious wrong, seeing pets neglected (pets that are abused) or someone has rushed in a pet who is critically sick, which makes our vets run late. They are working longer hours due to sick leave or just extended hours due to complex cases. In some practices, there is under-resourcing. This could be due to numerous issues such as staff being off sick or on leave, staff leaving the practice and/or walking away from the vet industry (giving up on their profession) that they once loved. This has left them feeling so depleted emotionally and mentally. Our vet teams need us more than ever now to support them, respect them and appreciate them. I am hoping this chapter will provide an insight to what our vet teams go through.

I can't stress enough the importance of having trust and faith in your vet team. This is paramount to your pet's care. If in doubt, there is no harm in getting a second opinion. Also, if you feel your current vet team is letting you down or doesn't have your pet's best interest at heart, look around for another vet team.

Word of mouth is a very powerful tool. As I previously mentioned in this book, up until Bear was around ten years old, I went to a previous practice where it was just about the money. I did my research, asked around, asked for recommendations on Facebook groups, and even did reviews. The only regret I have is not changing over to my local vet team sooner. I trust my vet team one hundred and ten per cent. I have that much trust and faith in the expertise and knowledge, that at no point do I ever need a second opinion.

I know in Bear's case they did everything they could and that unfortunately it was Bear's time. It is unfortunate but our pets are almost on loan to us, and they don't live forever. (If only they could.) I got to be with Bear when she took her last breath. She was surrounded by the very team that loved her as much as she loved them. They say a picture speaks a thousand words, and when I look at pictures of my vet team with Bear, I can see how much love she had for them and they her – it was genuine.

We start off bringing our pets to vet practices from kittens and puppies at such young ages, anywhere from six weeks old, and at times these vet teams deliver these kittens and puppies. We start the journey of our vet teams becoming another important person in our pets' lives. Our pets and vet teams become bonded with each other, and they think about the treats they are going to get. (LOL, I know Puss and Bear think like that.)

They are there for all the trials and tribulations. Bear did many a thing to land up at the vet, from splitting the side of her eye open to puncturing a deodorant can and eating many a thing a dog should not eat. I know my vet Michelle would have wished she could have fixed every possible ailment for Bear, as she knew how much Bear and I meant to each other. BUT, there are things our vets can't fix as much as they want to – things like heart disease, arthritis and cancer to name a few, all conditions that we as humans get. If only there was a magical pill that could keep them alive for as long as we live, but there isn't, and there is only so much our vets can do.

Let's think about this for a moment. This must take a toll on our vets. They haven't failed us, but at times they must feel like questioning themselves – could I have done more? Then comes the time they have to help us say goodbye to our beloved pet. They are expected to keep a straight face, not show emotion, but also at the same time are expected to comfort us. There wasn't a dry eye at the vet practice where Bear and I went, and if they didn't show emotion, I would be wondering why. Our vets have feelings and emotions just like any one of us.

Teams have their moments of crying with us, and some teams show the emotion then and there, but some teams try to be brave for us. That isn't to say that behind closed doors, once we leave the practice, they don't sob for us and for our pet that became their best friend. I could not do their job, but I hold them in the highest regard – they are my heroes. There is a saying that heroes don't have to wear capes to be just that. There are many unseen heroes each and every day, like doctors and nurses, but our vet teams also fit into this category.

When reading this book, the other takeaway I ask you to consider is to please be kind to your vet team. Acknowledge at times there may be a wait period due to a pet being rushed in as emergency.

Before you abuse a member of staff, stop and ask yourself these questions:

- If your pet was in urgent need of vet care, wouldn't you want or expect your pet to be seen urgently in front of others? How many urgent cases have come in where they have been required to save a pet's life?

- Has the vet, nurse or receptionist you're speaking with just helped console a person who has put their pet to sleep? They may have just spent extra time consoling someone. Think about this: when do our vet teams get to process their emotions when dealing with pets who have passed over? Nine times out of ten they are walking into the very next consultation, which might be you. Our vet teams not only form bonds with the pets but with us as pet parents, and in some cases they have watched these pets grow from the very first interaction at eight weeks old up until very old age in some pets.
- Before you go to abuse a staff member due to the cost of a procedure or treatment, wait time or the bad news you have just been given, take into account how you would feel, being them. They don't make up the costs and they certainly don't feel great giving people bad news. The vet team may have worked longer hours than anticipated to cover another staff member who has called in sick. They may not have had a meal break or toilet stop due to emergencies that have been rushed in. They didn't cancel your appointment with them due to someone calling in sick; they still manage to see everyone, no matter how much pressure this puts on them.
- Most of all, think about the pressures these guys face daily. How you act and what you may say might be enough to send this person over the edge. Many vets have committed suicide.

Treat everyone with humility and kindness. This goes a long way in a world that seems to be broken, where everyone thinks about themselves and doesn't have consideration for others. Not to mention how this pandemic has affected people. Each and every one of us has been affected in some way. Practices have become much busier. Think about the amazing work they do – they may one day save your pet's life.

If we don't speak up and support these amazing individuals, we will lose many more. This will then cause a knock-on effect. Practices will close due to under-resourcing (this has already happened in Mulgoa close to my home, and Parkes in regional NSW). Practices will close their books to new patients. We will have to drive farther for vet treatment and the costs will rise. But the biggest issue will be the knowledge and expertise. Some of these vet teams will not be able to be replaced by undergraduates. I have nothing against undergraduates – everyone needs to start somewhere – but undergraduates also learn on the job under the watchful eyes of these super-knowledgeable expert staff.

Let's also not forget about the amazing staff who work overnight in emergency vet clinics, and our vets and vet nurses who are on call. In country locations, we have vets who are on call to attend to livestock on farms and acreage (horses, sheep and cows). The vet teams go out in the middle of the night, early mornings in the freezing cold, snow, rain and windy weather to assist these pets and owners.

Before I end this chapter I would like to share a story in support of my above statements. On May 16th June 2022, I shared a post on my Facebook page – The Bear Project (credit to *PRIME News Central West*). They did a story about a vet (the only vet) in a town in regional NSW Parkes (country). There was only the one vet in Parkes. Due to resourcing issues, this vet has had to close its door permanently. The vet was emotional speaking about this. You could tell he loves what he does, but unfortunately he is unable to get vets and vet nurses and even undergraduates (in the past this was not an issue).

Due to the number of local vet practices needing vet staff, undergraduates were now able to get work closer to their home. The downside to this is the next nearest vet practice is in Dubbo NSW, which is around an hour and twenty minutes' drive from Parkes. Some of the practices in Dubbo have closed their books to new patients. This will make it a challenge for Parkes not having a vet in town, as now owners are going to have to drive some distance with critically ills pets to try and get seen by another vet. If we don't support our vets, we will have the same issues all over the state, not just in regional areas.

Our vet teams don't have to work in this industry – they choose to work in the industry as they love pets and making a difference in their lives. Our vet teams DO NOT deserve to be threatened, abused or be pushed to a point where they contemplate taking their own lives.

I feel like thank you is not enough for everything my vet team has done for me, especially with Bear and my other pets.

This chapter is a dedication to not only my vet team but to all vet staff, vets, vet nurses and reception staff who do an amazing job every day, and to acknowledge those that have lost their lives due to suicide and the pressures that the teams can sometimes face.

It is such a shame that we have lost some amazing people to suicide in this industry, which is something that should never have happened.

PLEASE if you are feeling vulnerable, please seek professional help.

A word from Bear's vet team

Vet Michelle with her beautiful Dachshund Molly

Bear's Vet Michelle Okorn

Michelle was Bear's favourite vet. Bear loved Michelle and I know Michelle equally loved Bear.

I've always wanted to be a vet. I'm sure that sounds like a cliche, but for me it's true. My mum tells me I knew what I wanted to do with my life from the age of five. I can't remember back that far; I just know that I've never wanted to do anything else.

I wanted to have a job that let me work with animals and with people. Not only that, I wanted to help animals and I wanted to help people. I've always loved animals (another cliché) and from a very young age begged my mum to let me become a vegetarian. I had the usual family pets growing up – cats, dogs, birds, fish. When I was in primary school, my dog, a cross Cairn Terrier named Scruffy, became really unwell for the first time in her life. We took her to our local vet clinic, and I was so worried about her – worried that we might be going home without her. I remember the vet examining her, explaining to us what was wrong and how she could be saved.

I couldn't believe it! A wave of relief and happiness and comfort came over me. I was in awe of that vet. But mostly, I remember thinking, "That's what I'm going to do!" I could help people feel this way. I could fix their pets and offer their families the same type of comfort I was feeling, knowing Scruffy was going to be alright. Scruffy lived until she was twenty-one years old. I was at university in my third year of veterinary science when she died. Three months later, longing for my own dog to love again, I got a puppy.

Molly, a ten-week-old smooth-haired, miniature Dachshund came into our home and filled up every corner of my heart. I didn't realise it at the time, but she would become my soul dog and teach me so much about being a vet and truly understanding the absolute depth to which someone can love an animal. As I write this, Molly is just over sixteen years old. Her life has been fraught with medical issues.

She has had spinal surgeries, anaphylactic reactions, food allergies, endocrine disorders, life-threatening drug reactions and now renal disease and canine dementia. There have been times when I've thought, "This is why I was meant to be a vet – to understand my own dog," and times when I've thought she's had all these issues so I can better understand what my clients go through.

Those clients that say, "This dog is my life, this dog is my baby, I can't imagine my life without them." I get it. Despite all her illnesses, Molly is amazing for a sixteen-year- old and she has a wonderfully spoiled life.

Seeing how much families love their pets and being a part of strengthening and lengthening that bond is one of the things I love most about my job. I love consulting. Being in that room with pets and their families is where I am the happiest. People love talking about their pets, and I love listening to their stories. Which may explain why I sometimes have trouble running to time ...

I love seeing the excitement when people bring in a new pet, and I love helping them understand how they can best care for them. I love seeing my regular clients and patients – it's nice to develop a familiarity with people over time. I also love the challenging medical cases – I still learn new things all the time. Medicine is changing and new advancements are made, but there are still diseases I have not seen and I am still amazed at how interesting the day can be.

For me, personally, one of the most challenging aspects of being a vet is how I can achieve the best diagnostic and treatment plan and outcome for my patient within the financial means of their owner, my client. I think some people find it difficult understanding the costs associated with a consultation, diagnostic testing and treatment or surgery, when our own health care costs are often supplemented by Medicare.

There is no Medicare for pets, and it unfortunately costs money to run a vet clinic so that clinics can continue to care for pets. I've had people tell me I don't care about their pet and I'm only in it for the money. If I wanted to make lots of money, I would've chosen a different profession. I don't pocket the vet bill and I don't work on commission. I really do care about your pet, a lot, and I also care about you and how you feel about your pet being sick. That's what keeps me coming back to work.

What I love the most about my job became one of the biggest challenges during the last two years with Covid: consulting. I found it really difficult moving from having families in the consult room with me, to having their pet brought in by the nursing team, examining their pet and then chatting to the client over the phone. It seemed much less personal. There are certain nuances during a face-to-face conversation that are simply missed during a phone consultation. Delivering bad news was also just awful over the phone. I imagine it was difficult for clients too, especially those with new pets or those new to our clinic – watching their beloved pet being carried or walked into the clinic, not knowing who the staff are or what the clinic looks like.

Are we being thorough despite no one watching? Is their pet scared without them? Did they really not cry for that injection? That's a lot of trust to be given and a privileged position to be in. One that was not lost on me at all. Another heart-breaking limitation of consulting during Covid is having to restrict the number of people that could be with their pet for a euthanasia. How do you decide who stays?

During Covid we also saw an increase in the number of people owning a pet. For a lot of the time over the last two years, these new pet owners, and existing owners, have been at home – forced to work from home, forced out of a job, in isolation, whatever the reason. There are more people with pets now with the ability to keep a closer watch over that pet, and perhaps with more time available to take their pet to the vet clinic. This situation was not coupled with an increase in the number of vets working in clinical practice. This exaggerated perhaps an already present issue – how do you fit everyone in?

A common thing I hear when I tell people I'm a vet is how much they wanted to be a vet but couldn't deal with putting animals to sleep. It's an inevitable part of the job. It goes without saying that no one likes it. It's something my ten-year-old self surely didn't think about when I was setting my hopes on being a vet. I still feel nervous walking into a consult, knowing that it's a euthanasia. Not because I don't feel confident about what I'm doing, but because each and every one is so different, with unpredictable moments from pets and people. And I want to make sure that each euthanasia is as smooth as possible, with as little stress to the animal and their family as possible. I am so aware that this is the last interaction those people will have with their beloved pet; I don't want it to be any harder on them.

I want them to walk away knowing that their pet was treated with love and respect, and given dignity to their last breath. I rely so much on the amazing veterinary nurses I work with. They help to keep me calm and focused, and they double and triple check that we have everything we need when we walk into that room. They ask if I'm okay afterwards. I couldn't do my job as well if not for them. I think for me, one of the hardest things is being surrounded by so much grief, and then often having to go on to the next consultation.

Everyone's reaction is different when their pet has passed. Some people sob silently and you can see their whole-body shudder, some people cry loudly, some people lie on the floor with their pet, some people hold back the tears until they've left the room. But the sadness is the same. For every euthanasia I walk into, I think about what had led these people to make their decision today. I think about what their pet means to them, and I think about the bond that they must have and how when they walk out of my room, they'll never get to hug them, or brush them, or pat them, or kiss them again.

I have cried in some euthanasia consults, especially the ones where I have known the pets for a long time. I've seen them grow up and watched their family grow with them. Sometimes I cry because I couldn't fix a pet – even when there is a diagnosis and we've reached the limitations of medicine, sometimes it still feels like a failure, and I wish there was more I could do. Sometimes I don't cry, not because I don't feel sadness or compassion, but because there are no tears left. Sometimes I hold back the tears and save them for later, because I'm also aware I've got other consultations to do and a waiting room filling up. I never hope for a euthanasia, but there are some euthanasia consults I hope I am present for. Clients and pets that I have a special bond with, and pets that I have known for almost their whole lives. I want a chance to say goodbye, but I also want a chance to support my client, maybe one last time.

Bear's vet nurse Crysten Hall

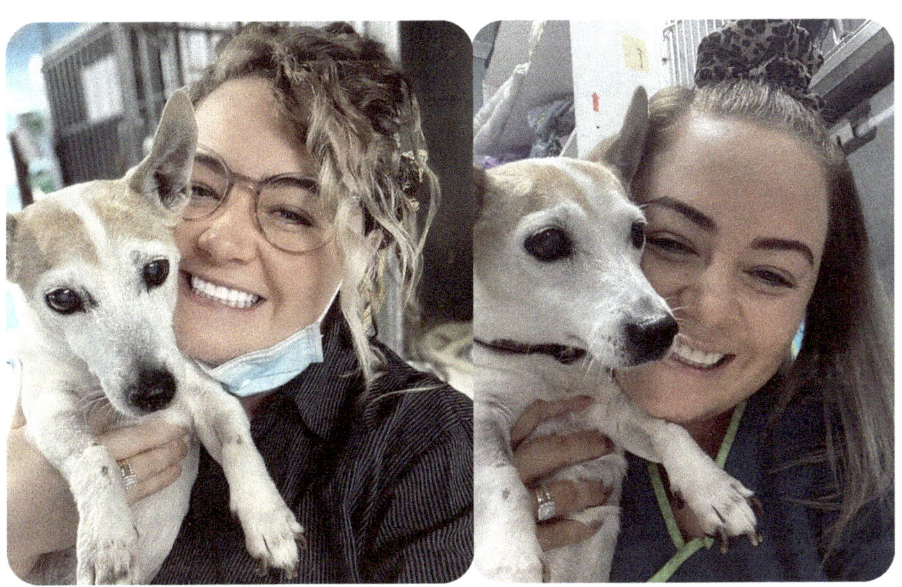

One of Bear's favourite vet nurses Crysten

My name is Crysten and I became a veterinary nurse to have a voice for those who don't, for those who communicate in a different way, to educate pet owners to better their pet's health and help fulfil a happy life between pets and their owners.

The thing I love most about my job is being there day in and day out for my patients and caring for them. Especially discharging that very sick patient who we thought was never going to make it – watching them walk out the doors with a wagging tail is everything! And of course, we aren't supposed to have our favourites, but when you get to know a patient and see them so regularly like Beary, you can't help but love them like your own!

As veterinary nurses, we endure extremely long days on our feet, witness animal abuse and rude, abusive clients and are told that we only care about the money and not their pet. This is definitely the hardest part of the job and one we struggle with mentally daily, and it definitely takes a toll on you after a while. It can get pretty rough!

The Covid period and being a veterinary nurse has been extremely difficult. Trying to fulfil clients' and patients' needs in a socially distant manner had its challenges, and we were busier, abused and run off our feet more than ever before! It has definitely been an adapting experience for all of our staff, but together we have made it work by building each other up, and that's all that matters.

Euthanasia tends to have a dark spot in the veterinary world and it is never an easy experience to be involved in, no matter how many you have been there for. As sad as a euthanasia is, I think we are so lucky we are able to send our beloved pets off before they have to suffer and struggle at the end of their life.

To be trusted to assist with sending a client's beloved pet over the Rainbow Bridge is always an honour, and I will always shed a tear. But to also see the instant relief in an animal's and client's eyes once they have crossed is also something that will always ease the pain in my heart for them and make me thankful that we can help ease and end their pain.

Bear's vet nurse Brooke Delaney

Another of Bear's favourite vet nurses

I started my career twenty years ago after leaving school in hospitality management. After years of serving people in five-star hotels, I found how hurtful people really could be for such trivial things. I always had a love of animals and decided to enrol in a TAFE course just to see if a change of career would help. Once enrolled, I never looked back, and loved every minute of study and interaction with my class, peers and teachers. I started my career as a kennel hand/junior nurse at a twenty-four-hour clinic.

Every day was different, with new animals and clients to meet and puzzles to solve. You tend to see people in a different light in the veterinary industry. One particular case I helped nurse for weeks was a very loved patient whose owner had cancer. His family thought if they could save the pet, they could save his owner. It was these situations that made me realise my change in career had a purpose.

I now felt like I was making a difference in people's lives by helping their animals, and this restored my faith in people, seeing them in a different light. I moved to general practice later in life, as the commute was too far and I was falling asleep while driving. It was here that I found a true family environment with staff members, clients and their pets. I looked after medical cases in hospital and also trained younger staff members. I had the privilege of being the delta dog instructor and visited many schools and preschools with my beloved dog, my best friend "Liberty" – Libby, my beautiful Cavalier.

One of the most rewarding jobs is knowing you are making a difference in teaching kids from a young age dog safety. The vet industry in general has become more challenging due to the impact of Covid. With more and more people working from home, pets have become very popular, as well as pet ownership, and pets have become more important in families' lives. Covid consulting with animals and nurses while owners waited in the car became the new normal.

Often, pet owners became very distressed due to sometimes not being able to see a vet as soon as they would like due to the large demand on vet services. It meant that if a patient or pet was stable, they might not have been able to see a vet for a week to two weeks.

This added to pet owners' anxieties and impacted the way they interacted with vet staff, who throughout the pandemic were showing up each day working to the best of their capacity – often while their young children were at school with other essential workers' children, and then going home to help their children complete their online learning. This was very challenging after being emotionally drained daily. With all this aside, it takes a certain personality to work in the vet industry. You need to be hardworking, understanding and empathetic, with a love of animals and people.

Sharlene Crofts talks about grief

Diesel *Ben and Diesel*

Hello, my name is Sharlene Crofts. I'm a counsellor and have my major in grief and loss.

I was honoured when Jody asked me to speak a little about grief and the loss of our pets and what it's like being pet parents – the grief we experience and loss we go through losing our pets. Our pets age much faster than we do, so they don't have as long on this earth. As pet parents, we love our babies and treasure every minute we have with them, and it never feels long enough sharing that time with them.

Our babies make a huge impact on our lives, whether they are a fish, a turtle or a dog, cat, bird or horse. We talk to them and bond with them and even though they can't converse and talk back, their love and actions show us they love us unconditionally. They don't ask for anything except for our love, food and water and of course a special treat here and there.

They give us three hundred per cent and save us from loneliness, sadness, the list goes on. Losing our babies is very hard. People have fear that if they open up about their grief, they will be laughed at or frowned upon or their feelings will be ignored. This should not be the case – we should be allowed to grieve like we do with any other loss.

Grieving takes time. We reflect on the times with our babies, and we have many mixed emotions – for example, happy, sad, angry, confused. We feel cheated and we are lost or numb, and some of us feel guilt. Whatever your feelings are, you're only human and it's very natural to feel what your feeling. We shouldn't have to hide how we feel; we need to process it, understand it and share what we are going through. Our self-care is paramount when losing a pet. We need to be kind to ourselves and know we did the best for our babies.

We need to reflect on the time we had with our babies to be able to heal. If we don't have this time, it takes much longer to heal. Some of us will feel our grief many years later and wonder why we are depressed or full of different emotions, as we didn't have or give ourselves time to grieve because we were not allowed nor given the opportunity to grieve. This is called disenfranchised grief. Many employers don't understand we need time off from work to deal with our grief. We should be allowed to have the same amount of time off as we would if it was a human we lost. It's part of our grieving process and healing. We go through the same process of grieving when we lose a human, and just because it's not someone close does not mean we are not extremely hurt or sad for the loss of our pets.

It's detrimental for our mental health to not have time from work to deal with our grief and loss of our babies. It's traumatic and it's not easy, and some of us may never get over that loss. We learn to live with it and adapt, but never get over it.

We lost our Rottweiler when he was eleven and a half years old. Diesel was six weeks old when we got him, and my special needs son, Ben, was six years old. They grew up together. Diesel was our family, not just a pet. When he passed away, I gave my five children time off from school and work to grieve the loss of our Diesel and to process that he had gone. I too took time off from my volunteer roles as I needed to process we'd lost our adorable big boy. It's been a couple of years and I still shed tears for his loss. If we hadn't taken that time off to grieve and have self-care, I feel we would still be in a sad, shocked state that he is no longer with us.

It's okay to feel what you're feeling, as our babies were a huge part of our lives. They helped us through so much, we shared so much with them and things we thought we could never get through, we did, as we had our babies with us. We need to give ourselves permission to grieve. We go through a journey and it's important for our well-being.

We need to give ourselves permission to grieve.

Some of us have only had our pets and no other contacts besides work or shopping. As pet parents, we involve our animals in almost every part of our lives, and to lose them we suffer immensely. If we are not given that time to grieve, it will affect us in the long term.

Connecting with our passed pets by Kelly Mercieca
Kelly's Animal Communication

Connecting to animals in spirit is one of my favourite types of communication sessions with animals. These sessions are truly incredible, and I am amazed by messages from the animals and the difference in how the owner feels afterwards. A lot of clients who book a session with me for their passed-over animal have had a traumatic or unexpected experience. The animals usually tell me that although things looked like they didn't go to plan, they went exactly to plan and that everything is okay. This is a huge comfort, and uplifting to their owner.

Kelly and her cat Comet

At such a difficult time, when many pet parents hold guilt over the events leading up to the passing of their pet, I find doing a session with the owner encouraging for the healing journey. Some pet parents just want reassurance their pet is not in pain anymore. The relief felt by the parents to be able to connect to their beloved pet through an animal communication session is so powerful for their healing journey. It enables the grieving owner to communicate a last message to their beloved pet and receive a message back. This whole experience for myself as an animal communicator is very fulfilling and so beautiful to be a part of.

Some passed-over animals may want to tell their owner what lessons or sole purpose they had to learn from each other. A beloved passed-over animal session provides the pet owner support in their healing journey from losing a pet. It can be soothing knowing they can still talk to them and are still connected by their hearts eternally.

Sessions with passed-over animals are about giving peace and comfort to the owners who may have not been able to say goodbye to their pet in the way they wanted to. One important thing to remember is each animal's and owner's journey is unique and there is no right or wrong in what each person has chosen. Most grieving pet parents want to know if they chose the right path for their pet with regards to euthanasia or letting them pass naturally. From my experience, we – including our animals – have chosen the path of our lives before we came to earth in our physical bodies, so the timing of when they leave is always right, even though it may be a traumatic experience.

Our beloved pets come to be with us here in the physical on earth for a time and have goals to achieve, but when they have completed their mission, it is time for them to leave their physical body and the earth plain. Although it is never easy losing a beloved pet, being able to connect to them in spirit is a magical way of supporting the grieving owner on their healing journey. Most animals tell their owners that they want them to be happy and to remember the good times they had. The animals in spirit don't want their owner to be sad, even though they miss their owner. The passed animals often have things they need to do on the other side.

To lose a pet can be harder than losing a human family member, and many clients can feel guilty about this until I assure them there is no need. It is understandable to feel such a loss when your pet has spent more time with you than most other people ever do. We tell our pets our secrets and they provide emotional and physical support. It is difficult to lose your best friend who slept next to you on your bed every night and whom you hugged when feeling sad or whom you took on walks every day.

We can feel a very deep loss with animals we have had a past life connection with, and it can be quite devastating for the owner to lose their best friend, their confidant. I am so blessed to support people through this journey. I have experienced the loss of pets personally, so feeling through my own experience and training, I am able to hold a special space and be there for my clients at a time when they feel like no one else understands them.

Often, no one else understands the pet owner's grief, and they love that I am able to hold space for them with no judgement. I am always compassionate to the owners' needs. Something else I often tell my clients is that there is no time frame for grieving. It comes in waves and they shouldn't feel guilty for feeling the way they do.

Their animals are always understanding and will say they were sad to leave their owner here on earth and will miss them very much, but they are usually leaving bodies that are not physically capable of moving like they used to, and that they feel so tired in. It is a relief for them to no longer have to deal with a physical body that they couldn't run or play in anymore.

A common question that owners have is if they will see their beloved pet again, and that is unique to each individual but, yes, I have had some animals in spirit say they may return if their owner doesn't stay on their path during this lifetime. Animals in spirit tell me they will be there waiting for their owner in many years when it is their owner's time to pass, and they will recognise them.

Animals who have crossed often tell me they will visit their owner in their dreams or at night when they may be drifting off to sleep or when they are having a quiet moment. Some animals choose to send messages through birds or other dogs that look like them so that we know they are still there with us in spirit. One message from a beautiful dog for his mum was really important because his mum wasn't there when he passed, and this was very painful for her and her husband. He told his mum she didn't let him down, and although it was hard, he wanted her to know it went according to plan and he wanted her to forgive herself. He told her she was not responsible and it was out of her control.

I connected with another beautiful dog who told me it was time for her to leave because her owner was moving on to their next phase of life, and they would be holding them back if they stayed here on the earth. It is so wonderful to connect clients with their animals in spirit, and although they are not here in their physical form anymore, it is a huge relief for the owner and very healing. Most clients tell me after the session they feel lighter, with a sense of peace, and it enables them to move forward more easily. This is a big part of why I do these sessions, to give some comfort to owners who are grieving.

It is important to keep an open mind and not have an expectation for what you receive prior to a session and trust that your animal in spirit will answer questions you ask and tell you what you need to know through me.

With love

Kelly Mercieca - Kelly's Animal Communication

Workplace Awareness

The purpose of this section is to raise awareness of grief in regards to the loss of a pet. I feel it is about time we are treated equally and fairly as pet parents, just like everyone else. I want to bring to the forefront the idea it's just a pet, and you can get another one. The people who say things like that, I truly feel sorry for. They have missed out on an incredible journey that a pet can take you on. Our fur babies are better than half the population in this crazy world.

Bear was my best friend in this crazy world, and we shared sixteen and a half years together. While living on my own, she was a true companion, but not only that, she was my medical therapy dog. Living with a *chronic* medical condition like Crohn's can be very isolating, and when they say a chronic medical condition, there isn't a truer word. I had experienced two miscarriages and I thought at the time they were so difficult, but they were nothing compared to losing Bear and what she meant to me.

She changed my world. When I had met Bear, I would never have realised back then how much she would change my life and how big an impact she would make on my life. She brought me happiness when I was a broken person, she taught me to love, open up to people and communicate on different levels. She also made me look at the world entirely differently. I am a better person because of Bear.

I believe there is a stigma attached to the loss of and grief for a pet within the workplace, and more awareness and understanding is required. Grief impacts mental health and well-being, and if a person is not supported and encouraged, this could lead them down a path of depression, PTSD and in worse cases, self-harm or suicide. Loss is loss, no matter whether it is a pet or a person. Keep in mind, a pet is all that a person may have. They may not have relatives or loved ones. They may live alone or suffer mental health issues, in turn making friendships hard to form. Elderly people can lose their lifelong partner, and if they didn't have children, a pet can become that person's lifeline.

In this day and age, particularly over the last few years, there has been a spotlight shone on mental health and well-being. I have a couple of friends who suffer with mental health issues but this is well managed. They work full time jobs and are under mental health care plans and have regular check-ups with health professionals. When they feel they are struggling, they reach out to friends and put a post on Facebook as their way of saying I need support. I have watched my friends at times struggle, but the support they have from family and friends has made a big difference. But, there are people who don't have that type of support network, and this is when they lean on a pet for solace, comfort and support.

There was a stigma attached to mental health in days gone by. People suffered in silence for fear of ridicule, judgement and for others to look down on them. I know this, as my own friends have faced it in previous years. Especially since Covid, the government has provided more funding for mental health and well-being. It is a very serious issue, and there are people out there now who are still scared to speak up or ask for help when they need it for the fear of ridicule.

Now, with the awareness of mental health, people's perceptions have changed. It is more acceptable and even encouraged to open up about one's struggles and face our demons. People's perceptions have only changed through raised awareness and people starting to talk openly about their struggles and share their stories. It takes a lot of courage and bravery for a person to speak up. When people speak up, that's when others in turn find the courage to speak up. Only when this happens is when awareness is brought about. The more awareness, the more society seems to be accepting and recognising there is an issue.

If we take a look at the past two years, Covid has left people isolated, cut off from friends and family members. There have been people stranded in other countries and the elderly not able to have visitors. This has also left people such as me who live alone, and the elderly who live alone, isolated especially when there were the 5 kilometre rules where you couldn't go out of your jurisdiction. When people like me who live alone are cut off from social networks, it becomes very challenging, leaving you feeling lonely and isolated. You can always speak to people on the phone and use Facetime or Zoom, but it isn't the same as leaving your house to visit someone, having a hug with a person or catching up for a lunch or dinner with friends.

If we look at the LGBTQIA movement, it took a long time for their voices to be heard, but they stayed strong, stayed true to themselves and fought for their rights and what they believe in (that they should be treated like everyone else). I mean love is love. It shouldn't matter about race, religion or sexual preference if two people love each other and are kind to one another. Why shouldn't they be allowed to marry and live the same as others? I ask the question why can't pet parents stand up for the same rights. After all, we are people, too, who have feelings, and love our pets unconditionally. Love is love, whether it is a person, child or pet.

I have even had the arguments with some friends that a pet and a child is different. The only difference to me is that a pet walks on all fours and can't communicate the same way a child does, and pet parents don't give birth. Would you say to a person who fosters or adopts that because you didn't give birth to that child your love is not as strong? I think not. However, any frequent guest in my home will tell you my pets communicate with me. I know what they are saying, what they want and when they are sick. The same goes for them. They know what I am saying and when I am sick. Only the other day, I had a friend visit for lunch, and she said, "When I walk into your home, I feel the love you and your pets have for one another." My pets actually have a better life than some children.

My friends are very supportive of me with my pets. I had one of my friends come over and stay for two days last year when I was in hospital. I created the pet bible for her. It contained all the information she needed to know, such as toilet time, treat time, breakfast and dinner, along with what time they needed to take their medications. My friends watched me battle at times, living alone and having Crohn's disease, and fully understand what my pets mean to me.

My view is a pet and a child are exactly the same!! Anyone who has pets, especially when they've taken them on from a pup or a kitten, knows you need to toilet train them, the same way you do a child. You have to socialise them with other pets, whether it be from your own home or others. This is the same way children go to preschool to learn how to socialise, play and share. You take them to the vet when they are sick the same way you take a child to the doctor when they are sick.

You rush them to after-hours vets, which could be anywhere from thirty minutes' to an hour's drive depending on where you live, the same way you would take a child to the hospital in the middle of the night when a child is sick. I have literally lost count of the number of times I had to take Bear and Angel to after-hours vets in the middle of the night for sickness. There really is no difference. The difference is what other people want to see as a difference. The only difference is we are not seen in the same light and given the same rights. Pets and pet parents are not recognised in the workplace, nor is there any form of bereavement leave or careers leave like there is for children.

When your pet has chronic medical conditions, there are constant medications. Over the time I have had all my pets, I have learnt there are a lot of conditions we have that our pets can get just the same, such as colitis, diabetes, seizures, epilepsy, heart conditions and skin allergies. They are even given human medication such as zyrtec for allergies, gabapentin for pain and anxiety, and flaygyl for colitis. When you break it down, I really don't see any differences between a pet parent and an ordinary parent. I do everything the exact same way an actual parent does.

In fact, I feel pet parents have more challenges. For instance, you really need to know your pets well. Pets can have off days just like we do. If you don't know your pet and their cues, you could be taking your pet to the vet every day, and this winds up to be costly. The other stressor is finances. Pets don't have Medicare, and they don't have public hospitals they can attend – everything is an out-of-pocket expense.

It can cost anywhere between two hundred and three hundred dollars just to walk in the door of an after-hours vet clinic, and that is before they start doing tests. Yes, there is pet insurance but this can work out very expensive, and at times you have to fight the claims. I have seen my friends have top cover for their pets, and they have had to fight the insurance company to receive their part of the claim back. Over the years, I have spent the best part of forty to fifty thousand dollars on vet care for Bear.

Why can't our workplaces change their policies? Why can't we have the same benefits as a parent? Why can't we have pet bereavement allowance? Why does there have to be that stigma in the workplace: it's just a pet – you can go out and get another one? What will it take for us to be looked at in the same light as other parents? We do exactly the same for our pets as parents do for their children. Why can't we be seen as another diverse group of people? I have had to take days off work to take Bear to the vet. I have used my RDO's and annual leave to look after them. Quite a few years ago, when Bear had her first knee reconstruction for a loose patella, I had to take four weeks' annual leave to stay home with her the entire time. I had to keep her confined to one room. I even slept on an air mattress so she wouldn't try and jump up on the bed.

I think now is the time more pet parents become courageous, and rather than be scared about the love they have for their pets, speak up. I think workplaces need to have a better understanding, greater awareness and more compassion for employees who are grieving the loss of a pet. When I took four days annual leave for Bear when she passed away, I told my manager I didn't want my work colleagues knowing why I was on personal leave. I was fearful of ridicule and of people saying, "It is just a dog – you can go get another one."

I know there are people in my workplace who don't understand. When you have lived your life with a pet for so long and they have become your best friend, your loyal companion and a health therapy dog, I am sorry, you can't just go and get another one, nor do you want another one. You want the one you lost – nothing can replace them. I was very lucky with my manager; she was very understanding, along with some of my bosses. However, I don't necessarily believe some of my other work colleagues would have been so understanding, nor some of the executives in the company.

When I lost Bear, I could barely get dressed and out of bed to eat, let alone rub two thoughts together. I felt like a part of me died with her. How was I meant to function and do my work? Impossible.

We now need to bring awareness into the workplace, especially now when mental health and well-being are in the spotlight. How do we do this?

We need to highlight awareness, start having the conversations, open up a dialogue and start being open about our feelings and how we are struggling with the grief. We can start with having support groups in companies rather than a company handing you a grief counselling phone number and advising you to call the number.

How about we start reaching out to our colleagues, start making it acceptable for pet parents to be okay with grieving rather than trying to hide it in fear of ridicule? Let that person take the time off they need to grieve the same way a person would to grieve for another person. Make the grieving person feel that it is okay to reach out and say they are not okay and need support. I have had people reach out to me and say their boss was horrible to them when they needed to take time off to grieve, and some of the reactions were shocking. I will touch on this later in my section on the polls I conducted.

1. My starting point to bring about awareness within my workplace was to put a post on Yammer, which is a platform within our company to talk about anything. Anyone within the company can see and post comments.

2. Start having conversations with other pet parents about their loss and their grieving. I knew I would not be the only one within my workplace going through this.

3. We have a team of Well-being Champions in my workplace – they touch on well-being subjects and support causes. I will be reaching out to them to see how we can get materials circulated within the company and see if we can organise a fundraising day for a local animal shelter.

4. Next is trying to change people's perceptions. I am one person; I can't change the world or even some people's perceptions, but I think starting the conversation is a good starting point. I was once told it takes a courageous and brave person to stand up and start the conversation, and then others will feel the same courageousness and join the army. It is like building an army – one person starts the conversation and then others will join. This is how movements are created, by becoming one and gaining momentum. You are always going to get people who are not going to jump on board with your cause or see things the way you do, and that is okay. Not everyone has to see things my way, but I think awareness is a good starting point.

5. Stigma. Changing this is extremely hard to do. You will still get people who are scared to speak up, as they fear they may get ridiculed just like I was and still am. I am still concerned I am going to get people responding in a negative way, but I also know there are others out there just like me. There is also stigma from others with comments like, "You just need to get over it. It was only a dog, you can get another one." I am now being courageous and putting myself out there. I am beyond caring about what others think of me. I was told by a very wise person that vulnerability can be the most powerful

commodity. I don't feel powerful but do feel extremely vulnerable doing this, but it is needed.

6. Possibly even a grief support group for pet parents (outside of work time).
7. If your company has a well-being or counselling service, the company could look at having a special Pet Bereavement Counsellor on board.
8. When we speak about diversity and inclusion, we need to include all groups, not just some. Indigenous, disabled and LGBTQIA are all now recognised and supported. Pet parents are another diverse group which is yet to be identified.

Here is the Yammer post I wrote on 21st January 2022:

"Calling all pet parents. Have you recently experienced grief due to the loss of a pet? I am working on a project and would love to speak with you. All details will remain confidential. Our pets have become such key members of our families, especially more than ever with Covid. Grief can be a traumatic experience as part of the process of losing our pets. Please reach out to me via email, I would love to hear from you about your experience."

At first, I felt there was a reluctance from staff to respond on the actual post, but by Tuesday 25th January, I had a couple of people reach out to me directly via email. This included men and women and the responses consisted of the same common theme – they felt like there was minimal to no recognition or support, as it wasn't seen as acceptable to discuss the loss of a pet, as it was not considered the same as a person.

Some staff didn't take time off and continued to work through the grief, as they felt it would be seen as unacceptable to take time off for the loss of their pet. Some felt their manager wouldn't understand. Other staff mentioned they felt there was a stigma. Some staff took sick leave and annual leave, as they felt this was easier to do rather than try to explain what they were going through. As shown by the responses I have received, these pets were family to these staff members, but they were suffering in silence due to the lack of awareness of grief around the loss of a pet.

The people I spoke with on the phone and via email all had different stories of their pets – why they wanted a pet, how their pet helped them and how their pet passed away. The one common theme we all had was the love for our pet, what our pets meant to us, how they were treated like any other family member and how their pet helped them in many ways. The grief and the loss affected us in the same manner.

When I spoke to other staff at my workplace, the strongest theme every staff member commented on was the lack of support and awareness in the workplace. They mentioned they would love to see changes made and felt it was well overdue that someone was speaking out. I feel there is a very big gap within the workplace and that changes need to be made. I feel I need to be an advocate in the workplace for people like me and for our pets.

If we look at a tree, for example, the trunk represents our core (our mental health and well-being) and the branches represent the daily stressors and challenges we face (as depicted by the below diagram).

Most of the branches are known and recognised within the workplace. The workplace acknowledges these challenges and offers help and support to employees. In this day and age, most of these challenges are spoken about and encouraged to be discussed, and support is provided.

There is one branch missing - Grief In Relation To The Loss Of A Pet

However, most workplaces don't recognise the loss of a pet. When a staff member loses a loved one, there is empathy from other work colleagues and senior managers. Work colleagues rally around and say things like, "I am sorry for your loss," "Is there anything I can do to help?" "If you need a chat, please reach out," "Take all the time you need." When a pet passes away there is not necessarily this level of support from work colleagues and in some cases no empathy or even acknowledgement.

At the time of printing this book, I am in the early stages of starting to have conversations with staff and senior management about more awareness needed within the workplace. In a way, it was comforting for me to realise there were others within the company where I work who felt exactly how I was feeling, and who also felt more awareness was needed in the workplace. Why are we suffering in silence? Is it fair for a person to suffer due to feeling ridiculed or not understood?

The loss of a pet and the loss of a person is exactly the same, with the same impacts, so why, as pet parents, should we feel ashamed of the love we have for our pets? Once upon a time, people who suffered with mental illnesses suffered in the same way – too ashamed to speak out in case people ridiculed them and didn't understand what they were going through. That gap has started to be bridged – a new light has been shone. Because of the bravest of people who are courageous enough to speak up and say this needs to be spoken about, we are now bridging the gap on mental health and well-being. Grief is a part of mental health and well-being. It needs to be acknowledged and people need to be supported. It should no longer be acceptable that because it is a pet it is deemed as different and not recognised.

Pet parents need to be brave and courageous and speak up about the love and bond they have for their pets, which is how we will start the conversations and bring about awareness. This is a very hard thing to do, however. I must admit I feel very vulnerable speaking about this and know there will still be people out there who don't understand and can't appreciate my point of view. It is particularly hard to be vulnerable to an entire workforce/your colleagues, this leaves the door open for people to ridicule and judge you. However, I don't care what people's perceptions are of me.

Bereavement for pets in the workplace is not recognised. I would like to see this changed and for us to be given the same rights as people with children. It is acceptable for parents with children to take time off to go to concerts and assemblies and when children are sick. Why can't pet parents be afforded the same privileges? Imagine being one of the first companies to bring in a policy specifically for pet parents, including bereavement. This could set a precedent for other companies. It could make you a more desirable workplace with more content staff. Staff could look at this company as a place they want to work. It could also shine a spotlight on your company as a good news story on social media platforms such as Facebook. Happy, content, supported staff show greater production in work and a greater commitment to the company.

Staff would be more forthcoming about why they needed to take time off, rather than to lie. As I mentioned earlier, I have been very fortunate with my manager – she has been very understanding and supportive. When Bear passed away, she rang me every day for a week to see how I was doing and to just let me chat and cry. I feel very grateful for this. But more workplaces need more supportive senior management.

Since Covid commenced in March 2020, there has been an increase in pets being adopted and purchased. More families have welcomed a fur baby into their home, whether it is a dog, cat, bird, or rabbit. Most families now have some type of pet. This has been great for animal shelters and animal welfare leagues, as it has meant fewer homeless and abandoned pets. This has also brought about a heightened awareness that pets can become part of the family, whereas a family may not previously have thought about taking on a pet.

Covid brought with it so many challenges – I don't think a single person during this time has not suffered some sort of hardship or loss from Covid. This could range from financial loss to mental health issues, family members passing away and family not being able to attend funerals, the elderly not having visitors, whether it be in a nursing home or their own home and those like myself who live alone. Covid has affected everyone's life in one way or another, and some people more than others.

I was fortunate enough to keep my job and work from home, but living and working from home brought about a new challenge for me – no social interaction. This was especially heightened during lockdown when we couldn't visit friends. Normally, on weekends, I see my friends and have lunch or dinner with them. This now was non-existent. Although being in lockdown and working from home left no social interaction, I was very lucky in the sense that I had my pets (five at the time – two dogs, a cat, a rabbit and a horse).

They kept me busy, but also kept me going. I relied on them for mental stimulation and would play ball and tug-of-war, and was even at times able to take them for a walk. Having a chronic medical condition puts me in the vulnerable category, so even when lockdown was lifted, I was still extremely cautious about where I was going. I relied on my pets for comfort, solace and support when the world seemed to be in chaos. The pandemic took over, but the one consistent component of my life was my pets.

It should never be underestimated what a pet can actually mean to a person and how they can be there for a person mentally and emotionally. If we look at the elderly who live on their own in their own home and have lost their partner (husband or wife), they may have a pet. If so, that pet is often the only thing they have that keeps them going. The pet offers that person comfort, reassurance and companionship, making them feel less alone. It can also protect them by alerting the elderly person if someone is around. Our pets can be our biggest protectors, who are very intelligent, loving and loyal.

I recently stumbled across an article about a homeless man and his dog. This is the story of John and Carrie who lived around central station and George Street, Sydney.

A homeless man and his dog give a glimpse into what it's like to live rough!

John and his dog Carrie had been living rough in Pitt Street Mall and on the streets of Sydney. John had attempted many times to find a bed and a place to stay, but none would accept pets. Rather than give up his dog, John continued to sleep on the streets. This is a perfect example of a pet and human bond. He loved Carrie so much he would rather be on the street with her than be in a comfortable bed off the street. A bond between a human and a pet should never be underestimated. For John, Carrie was all he had. He was completely devastated when some young boys kicked Carrie and she ran away. Many people got to know him and would buy him coffee and bring food for Carrie. One complete stranger, Debbie Organ, offered rewards for the safe return of Carrie. Carrie was found and returned to John the very next day.

One day, this lady introduced herself to John and rang organisations to find out why he couldn't be offered any form of accommodation for himself and his little dog. She advocated for him and stressed that pets are like family, and all three organisations told her it would be easier to put the dog down. How one complete stranger changed a homeless man's life:

Dog Lover's Care Saved Homeless Man – Pals in a new leash of life!
By Debbie Organ

WHEN Debbie Organ helped rescue the dog of homeless man John, neither of them knew it would be the beginning of a friendship that would ultimately save his life.

In 2013, John was beaten up while sleeping rough in Sydney's CBD, prompting his fox terrier Carrie away in terror. Ms Organ — who saw John regularly on her way to and from work in Pitt Street Mall — learned of Carrie's disappearance and posted a reward online. Before long, she found Carrie and returned with the dog to introduce herself to John. The two became friends.

"Initially it was the dog (that compelled me to act) because I'm a big animal lover, but then I sat down to talk to John," Ms Organ said. "People would come up and say hello to him, but one day there was a very good looking young man in a suit who started swearing at me in the middle of Pitt Street Mall, saying 'you're encouraging homelessness by sitting with this idiot' — and then John stood up to protect me."

In 2017, John had a fall and was rushed to hospital in a critical condition. He needed surgery but, with no legal guardian to give consent, doctors could not operate. Once again Ms Organ — and Carrie — came to the rescue. Ms Organ's number was on Carrie's collar and when a stranger found the dog alone she was called, triggering a search for John. Eventually, Ms Organ found him in Royal Prince Alfred Hospital. "John had nobody to sign his consent forms and body to care for him. So, I had to become his legal guardian", she said. "I went through the guardianship process. They weren't sure he was of sound mind — he's much better now."

For her selflessness, Ms Organ has been nominated for a Pride of Australia award.

John recovered after his operation and Ms Organ helped him find accommodation in a Belrose nursing home near her house in Frenchs Forest.

Credit – article by Debbie Organ, article taken from Integrity Corporate Finance Group.

The pet industry has soared in the last two years, and vets are busier than they ever have been due to a lot more families now having pets. At a time when businesses were closing down, pet stores were thriving. Even at times you couldn't go into the store due to lockdown, you could click and collect or have the products delivered.

In the last couple of years in particular, companies and businesses have started to see there is a real need for them to open up their facilities for pet parents and families. You can now take your pet on vacation with you. There are many hotels, Airbnb's and villas where your pet can stay on site, and you can have your pets in the accommodation with you.

There are also pet-friendly cafes where you can eat in with your furry companion. They even have pet menus with doggie ccino's. These businesses are genius. They saw a real market for this and an opportunity to open up the business to everyone. As a pet parent, if I was to go on holiday, my pet would come with me and these types of businesses are the ones where I will choose to stay and spend my money. Any business that recognises pet ownership and is supportive of pet parents will get my business and interest more so than others. Why is it that so many cafes, pubs and holiday facilities are welcoming of pets but yet our workplaces are not?

Why can't our workplaces see a need for a pet bereavement policy and awareness?

Covid gave us a heightened sense of mental health and well-being. If pet parents are not supported and given the understanding and time to grieve, and are expected to go about our life and work, how does this help our well-being and mental ability to function, let alone do our jobs? Covid or no Covid, grief is very real and very debilitating.

There are many support groups on Facebook for the loss of a pet. I have joined a couple of these groups and found the outpouring of love and support truly touching. There are so many people like myself from all over the world going through the same emotions and feelings, which says to me workplaces need to get on board with awareness and make changes to workplace policies. There is a real issue and a real change is needed and needed now.

I recently did some Facebook polls in a couple of the groups, and I did advise people that none of the names or details would be listed here for privacy purposes. I did mention I would be including comments, but once again, no names of companies, states or people.

The feedback I received was pretty overwhelming. I had quite a few people reach out to me via instant messenger and will detail some of my findings below:

One of the questions I asked was, "Do you feel your workplace was supportive when you lost or grieved the loss of your pet?" Another question I asked was, "Did you tell your workplace the reason why you needed to take time off work for the loss of your pet?"

- It appears that smaller companies have more compassion and understanding for a person who has lost or is grieving for a pet. Some even sent flowers and cards to their employees and rang in to make sure they were okay. They were also understanding of taking time off work. Small workplaces seem to treat their staff like family, rather than just a number or a bum on a seat.

- One lady messaged me and not only told me her company did the above, but paid her, not from annual or sick leave. She wasn't aware if they had some type of pet policy but they paid her for five days off work.

- A lot of people said they didn't feel they were supported by the workplace and that bosses couldn't understand why they needed to take time off for the loss of a pet. One lady told me when she asked to take time off, her boss replied with, "What? Are you kidding? It's just a dog." She said she was even more distraught.

- Another person told me her boss was not understanding and even gave her the silent treatment when she returned to work. She lost another pet within six months, but this time she made up a medical reason to take time off, as she said she didn't want to experience what she had previously. She told me soon after this she found another job due to some ridicule from fellow colleagues. She said it was almost like they were making fun of her because she was grieving for her pet.

- A lot of people said they felt like they would be ridiculed by senior staff and other work colleagues, so they tried to keep working as best as they could, or just called in to work sick, as they didn't think their workplace would be supportive.
- I also received quite a few responses where it seems to come down to the individual manager as to how people are treated. One lady told me that when her cat of eighteen years passed away, her manager hugged her, cried with her, sent her home and told her to take the next few days off. There were quite a few of these stories that seemed to shine through. I was reading these and crying my eyes out. When you lose your companion, a simple thing like a hug can be comforting, along with understanding.
- Another person told me he worked for a very big corporation. The day after he lost his pet, he went to work and mentioned it in a meeting with his big boss and other colleagues. There was silence for about a minute, and he said not one person asked him if he was okay, and then they continued on like nothing had been said. No one had even noticed he left the building every day at lunchtime to go and sit in his car and cry for the duration of his lunch break.
- Another person mentioned he also worked for a big corporation (he and his wife worked together at the same company). His wife's cat had been run over just near their house that morning when they were about to leave for work. Her cat was like her baby – it meant everything to her. When she saw the cat, she was completely shattered. He rang work to say she wouldn't be in and he also wouldn't be in. He said his boss's tone of voice was appalling when he said, "So, she isn't coming into work today?" The husband said, "No, and

neither will I." The boss then replied with, "You're kidding, right? You are also not coming in?" The husband said, "No, I will not be in, I can't leave my wife like this, she is completely distraught."

As I have mentioned, I am on a couple of grief loss pages and they all depict the same sad stories, how the person's pet meant everything to them, their heart is breaking and they don't know how they are going to continue. I can see anywhere from twenty to fifty posts a day on the grief loss pages (that is just one support group).

Grief doesn't only affect women but also men, your children and other pets. I have seen grown men break down over losing their pet. Men seem to feel comfortable around others going through the same thing (mainly on the grief loss pages). One man had recently said on one of the pages he feels at ease being able to talk about his sadness and grief, as the people on this page understood.

One of my friends lost his cat over five years ago. This cat was like his child, and five years on, he said he still tears up to this day when a memory or a trigger makes him think about his cherished fur baby. I think it is beautiful, especially for a man to be able to speak openly about this. These are the types of conversations we need to be encouraging, not belittling.

Men are programmed to be strong and detached from their emotions – it's not considered manly to cry, let alone over a pet. There is a stigma around men being emotional and openly speaking up about the loss of their pet, which I feel needs more acceptance and encouragement for them to do so. Why should they suffer in silence? Why should they feel ashamed or embarrassed?

PTSD (Post-Traumatic Stress Disorder)

One lady in the group mentioned in her post that her two pet dogs escaped from the front entrance of the home and ran straight across the road into the path of an oncoming car. She watched on helplessly as both dogs were hit by the same car and died right in front of her very eyes. She has been so traumatised by this event that she has been under the care of a psychologist who has since diagnosed her with PTSD.

What is PTSD? PTSD is a psychological medical disorder that develops in people who have experienced an extremely traumatic event or a string of traumatic events. It can bring about fear, anxiety, anger and depression. They feel almost paralysed by the event, which can then cause triggers in life. This can affect a person physically, mentally and emotionally. Some people live with this for many, many years, if not forever.

PTSD can cause disturbed feelings with distressed thoughts. The person may have constant flashbacks, nightmares about the event and may feel constant sadness, fear and anger, and disengage themselves from family and friends. This condition can be debilitating and can last for months, years or even in some cases for the rest of the person's life.

As psychologist Julie Axelrod has pointed out, the loss of a dog is so painful because owners aren't just losing the pet. "It could mean the loss of a source of unconditional love, a primary companion who provides security and comfort, and maybe even a protégé that's been mentored like a child," she writes for Psych Central.

Credit – Dr Julie Axelrod, quote taken from Why Losing a Dog Is So Painful, According to a Psychologist (yahoo.com)

The loss of a pet can be very devastating and traumatic. The human bond that develops with a pet is a long-lasting attachment, which is broken with the loss of a pet. However the pet has passed on, the death of a pet is traumatic and the distress exhibited by the owner can display symptoms of PTSD. Some of the symptoms are outlined below:

- Nightmares
- Anger
- Memory loss
- Negative / intrusive thoughts
- Disengaging from family and friends – avoidance in social scenarios
- Concentration issues
- Hypervigilance
- Not being able to sleep
- Flashbacks

Grief and the loss of a pet is very debilitating, and it is about time workplaces became more aware and more supportive of employees experiencing grief. It is not good enough that we advise a staff member to seek counselling. It is better still to reach out to that employee and be supportive. Sit down with them, let them talk about their experience, ask them what you can do to help support them through this difficult time and show care and genuine sympathy. To that person, their whole world feels like it has changed. It is not right that a person should feel they need to suffer in silence.

WORKPLACES, LET'S START THE MOVEMENT TO SUPPORT STAFF WHO ARE GRIEIVING OVER THEIR PET.

LET'S LOOK AT WORKPLACE POLICIES – INCLUDE THEM, NOT EXCLUDE THEM. PET PARENTS ARE ANOTHER DIVERSE GROUP WHICH IS YET TO BE RECOGNISED.

LET'S MAKE IT ACCEPTABLE TO TALK ABOUT THE LOSS OF A PET.

LOOK AT INCLUDING OUR PETS UNDER A POLICY FOR PAID LEAVE UNDER COMPASSION (SAME AS A PERSON)

How can workplaces raise more awareness and acceptance?

Workplaces need to have accountability for their staff. It is called a duty of care. It should not be deemed acceptable to provide someone with a counselling number or suggest this and just keep moving on about daily business. Who knows, this person could be struggling greatly with their grief and reaching out for support. By turning a blind eye, this could be enough for someone to self-harm, or in severe cases, commit suicide. When people become desperate for help, they may not be thinking rationally. Now is the time to reach out to staff and support them rather than have them suffer in silence – how is that fair to a person? Should anyone be made to feel like that? Grief comes under duty of care.

When I talk about bereavement leave or policy, this could be as simple as not necessarily creating a new policy, but INCLUDING bereavement for pets under an already existing policy such as compassionate leave. Workplaces have so many different types of leave, such as compassionate leave, careers leave, rostered days off, annual leave and so on. This could quite simply be included under an already structured leave (such as compassionate).

Bereavement leave for a pet doesn't mean they will be taking a paid leave every year (multiple pets would need to be considered), but would only be a paid day or two when the pet passes away. This would be treated in the same way as when a staff member loses a person in the family.

During my time speaking to staff within my workplace, there was only a small group of people (fifteen), but I know there are more out there who could be afraid to speak up or may be going through the grieving process and finding it hard to talk about it. They could even struggle with talking to a stranger (another work colleague) in case of the stigma.

Companies could use a marketing strategy which shines a light on the company in a positive way. Not only highlighting that happy employees feel more productive in the workplace, are more content and less likely to leave, but they would be less likely to lie about taking time off to grieve.

Companies could raise awareness and organise a fundraiser for their local animal shelter as simple as a one or two dollar coin donation. Senior management could attend the shelter and provide the funds and run a social media story. Not only does this raise awareness and funds for a shelter but also provides a good news story for the company, which they could share on social media. When you look at all the examples, this is a WIN WIN for everyone involved. The only drawback is we can't have our pets back.

Also, by being a pet parent-inclusive company, this could make a company a more desirable employer. I know if I was looking for a position and saw that in an advertisement, it would grab my interest, and I would be keen to work there knowing they have an understanding of the importance of pets.

There are so many opportunities to raise awareness on this very important subject that is currently sitting in the dark behind closed doors whilst a lot of people suffer in silence. Companies can no longer fall short in this area and not see potentially disastrous consequences for staff.

Years and years ago, pets were treated as that. They were mainly kept outdoors and not really seen as part of the family. They were fed scraps from the table and left outside in the weathered elements. Nowadays we have a lot of pets in TV commercials, people buy designer outfits for their dogs and cats and some pets have just as many outfits as people. Pets celebrate Christmas and have photos with Santa (mine did every year for the past five years). Pet parents even throw birthday parties for their pooches (I have been to some). Children and pets are all welcome, and to be honest, they are joyous events. Our pets sleep indoors, go to dog parks and some pet parents take their doggies to doggy daycare for the day while they are at work. They go on vacations with families and to cafes for lunch. Why is the workplace so far behind?

While writing this chapter of my book, one of my big hopes and aspirations is that team leaders, managers, senior management and execs will read this and see this as a real opportunity to support pet parents. I would love for them to take something away from this chapter, and that is to be a driving force within their own company to help build change and inclusion around our pets and us as parents.

Jody Crossley with her dog Angel and horse Sunny. Photo: Melinda Jane.

EMILY FESZCZUK

Jody Crossley was plunged into a deep state of grief after her 16-year-old Jack Russell named Bear died last year.

Writing about her raw emotions to help her heal, the Glenmore Park resident now wants to release a book on grief and help break the stigma that surrounds losing a pet.

"I live alone and have Crohn's disease and Bear was very in tune with my medical condition... she wasn't a dog to me but more the child I never had," Ms Crossley told *Weekender*.

"Bear was the first pet I got as an adult, so I was looking for a book to give me some sort of validation of what I was feeling when I realised there was a gap for one from a personal perspective."

With 48,000 words written, Ms Crossley said *The Bear Project*, as she has named it, grew into a bigger body of work.

"I have an amazing vet team so I added a chapter about the pressures of having to put an animal to sleep and then go to the next consult, so when is there time for them to process their emotions?" she said."

"My counsellor friend has written a chapter and I have five pet parents who have gone through the grief stage share their own stories about how they dealt with it."

Ms Crossley is trying to raise money to get her book published, which she hopes will be the catalyst for change in the community.

"I have a quote of $10,000 from a consulting company to edit it, publish it and get it out there, so if businesses come on board, we will have a sponsorship page and share their details on social media platforms," she said.

"The book is the first step, but I am also trying to build momentum for workplaces to acknowledge and start supporting people who lose pets that play such an important part in their lives."

The NSW Government offers leave that can be used for the death or illness of a close member of the family, but it does not extend to pets.

The NSW Department of Premier and Cabinet did not provide a comment about whether it would consider a policy in workplaces for pet related grief.

To donate to *The Bear Project*, call Jody on 0402 254 443 or email jodycrossley@hotmail.com.

Credit – Western Weekender Friday March 11, 2022 – article written by Emily Feszczuk, photo by Melinda Jane. This was the first media source to believe in my story and the journey I am trying to achieve by helping others.

PART 3

Stories of grief from other pet parents

Garfield

A CAT'S STORY – By Mark and Julie Kendrigan

Well, it all started with a trip to the pet shop in Mt Druitt Shopping Centre, where my wife Julie and I were looking for a cat to bring home, and guess what? We found two. A ginger and white cat we named Garfield, and a black and white cat we named Casper. Casper went to our son's house, and we kept Garfield. Well, Garfield was a fifty-five dollar pet, but he had the personality of a millionaire.

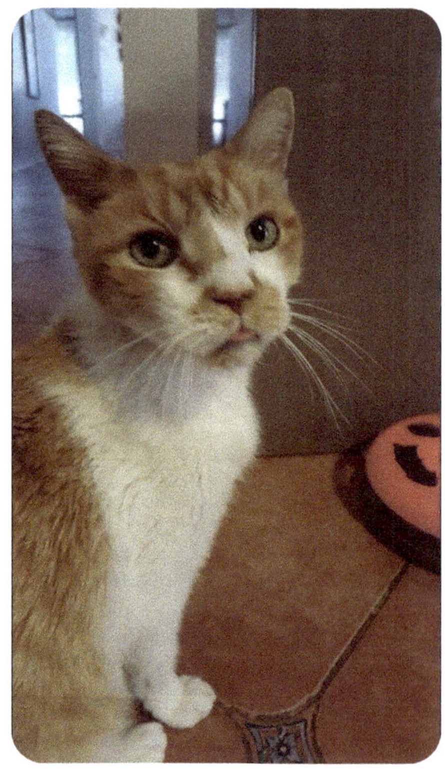

This was Garfield's pose – tongue hanging out.

Garfield was the first animal I had owned since I lived with my parents, so he was special. He could make you laugh, he could make you cry and he was a joy to all. Now, from day one Garfield was not a normal cat.

He couldn't eat the same brand of food every day, as it would make him have bowel problems. He didn't meow, he would like cough, but not a cough – a very strange sound, but you knew that every inflection would mean something.

Brushing a cat can be dangerous if they don't like it, but not Garfield. He stands, sits and lies down for a brush. He had short hair and we have videos of how much hair we got off him (it made a litter of kittens), and he would keep coming back for more. Also, he had very little balance, so he fell off tables and chairs. I don't know why, he just did.

When anyone would turn up – friends, tradesmen – he would want a pat or a scratch. He was afraid of nothing. He also told the tradesmen what to do. When it came to feeding him, he was a Garfield. He would eat like a pig and then throw it back up again and then go back to the bowl for more. So my wife decided to call him away after a while and make him sit for about five minutes until he burped. Then he was told he could go on eating and that seemed to work.

Above all, Garfield was a mother hen. We brought home a kitten that was found in my friend's backyard, and Garfield mothered him like a female would. We had Garfield for fifteen and a half years till he got really skinny, but he was still eating and pooing, and then one day he stopped eating and we tried to hand feed him kitten food. He would lick it off my hand and then ten minutes later he would throw it up. We took him to the vet and they did a blood test and couldn't find anything, so they gave him a needle to stop him vomiting, but it didn't work.

Then my wife and I talked about our mission – if they couldn't help him and they couldn't get him eating again, we would have to put him to sleep. We took him back and the vet had made a list of more than twenty injections that could help and maybe give him three months or maybe kill him, so we decided to put him to sleep.

I'm 125 kgs and not a blokey bloke, but you hurt me and I will hurt you back. But, when they gave Garfield that green needle, I was a mess, crying and sobbing, and then my wife was also crying – we must have looked a sight. I will tell you now, we cried for three days, and when we got his ashes, we cried again and again, just like I'm doing now.

Garfield has been gone six years on the 5/4/2022 and we still miss him, we still talk about him and we still cry over him. Grief is something you can get over, but it will always return when the subject of Garfield comes up.

Love from Mum (Julie) and Dad (Mark)

Archie

By Kym Smith

I was just going through the motions. I eat, work, sleep and repeat. That's it. No hobbies, no interests, nothing. A childless woman just drifting. I'd had my fair share of assholes, and they left me mentally scarred. Scarred to the point I had to check the lock twenty times a day, always looking behind me. Always keeping watch, ready to run, always on high alert. It was an automatic response after years of trying to leave a controlling, abusive relationship. It culminated with a house fire and attempted murder charges. The coward took the easy way out before the trial and God was his judge.

It wasn't easy not living in fear anymore. I was drained. I moved on but I was empty, and Archie came at a time when I needed him the most. His family was moving interstate and they just couldn't take him with them. They loved him for the first two and a half years of his life and I promised them I would love him for the rest.

I'm not going to lie, for the first six months with us, Archie missed his previous family. He wouldn't bark and he would wait at the gate, looking out at the driveway. It broke my heart, so I gave him space and I did what he loved the most, playing his version of fetch. I would throw him the ball and he would make me run around trying to get it back. It was his most favourite game, and I must have been really good at it because one day, my brother came to visit and he let out the biggest bark. I was so happy he was finally home.

So, from then on, he made sure he protected his home. One day, I heard a clinking sound, like someone was opening a gate. I said to my husband, "Can you check who's there?" Before we knew it, Archie scrambled off the couch, out the doggy door and ran to the gate barking. My husband and I looked at each other stunned; he understood us.

He understood a lot of things, but "drop the ball" wasn't one of them. He was insanely smart. When we bought a new couch, we told him it was the only place he couldn't sit. He could go anywhere and lie on anything, but not the new couch. Every morning when we woke up, we found him sleeping on his bed next to the couch. "What a good boy," we would tell him. "You've listened to us."

One night, we were in bed and my husband went to get a drink of water. He came back and said, "Archie has been sleeping on the couch." He told me he heard a rustling noise coming from the lounge room, and just as he entered the room, he saw a shadow moving. When he turned on the lights, Archie was in his bed but the leather couch was warm and my husband could see indentations in it.

Well played, Archie, well played. So, after that, we put a throw rug over the couch and Archie claimed it as his. No more pretence, you've got us, it's yours. For years, he slept on that couch. I guess it was because it's near the doggy door and he could hear the goings on outside. Whatever the reason, I felt safe with him close. Archie was my shadow, my constant companion. Wherever I went, he was right behind me. I couldn't imagine life without him.

We would go for a walk every day around our local lake. Despite living on acreage, he loved going there and having a good sniff. One Sunday afternoon, I was feeling a bit lazy and didn't really want to go for a walk. I just wanted to hang around and watch Bridgerton, but Archie gave me that look. "Come on, it's walk time." I just couldn't deny him. So we went on our usual walk, and he sniffed until his heart was content.

The next morning, I noticed he was limping a bit when he got up from his bed. I thought it was his arthritis playing up, as we took him to the vet a couple of months prior, and she thought he had arthritis. By that evening, his right leg had started to swell and we rushed him to the vet hospital. After multiple tests and CT scans, he was diagnosed with hemangiosarcoma. The specialist told us the only way to treat it was to amputate his leg, and it would buy him anywhere between two to five months.

It was such a devastating blow, but I knew in my heart a three-legged German Shepherd wouldn't be able to cope when all he wanted to do was play fetch and run around free. As much as I wanted to keep him a couple of months longer, I just couldn't let him suffer. We made the difficult decision to let him go. I held him in my arms, and I told him he was the best dog and that I loved him. That I still needed him and that he couldn't go anywhere yet. I will never forget the pain of walking out of that hospital. I cried until there were no more tears left. I was beyond devastated.

That evening I was driving back home from McDonald's. I guess I just wanted to stuff my face with a Big Mac to make myself feel better. It didn't. As I turned onto our road, the gum trees parted and I looked up at the sky. I saw a dog in the clouds, prancing against a red sunset. In that moment, my tears dried. The pain eased and I knew that I was going to be okay. My boy was telling me he was okay, that he's still around. I just needed to look out for him.

Since his passing, I noticed things I haven't seen before, like a blue fairy wren greeting me as I got out of the car to take his fur sister for a walk. A butterfly flying in my face when I was thinking about him. Or the butcherbird that landed next to me, singing.

Three years ago, I attended a doggie birthday party with Archie. (Yes, I'm that person). My friend gave me a Queen of the Night cutting. She told me the flowers will bloom only at night, for one night, once a year. Over the years, I have only ever seen a wilted flower. Somehow, I kept on missing it bloom and haven't seen a flower from it.

Recently, I was outside in the garden, and I noticed a few buds and thought maybe this time, this time I might see it bloom. I stayed outside, I counted nine buds and I suddenly realised that it was the 21st. For, you see, the 21st of October was when my boy passed away. My boy sent me a flower, one for every year he spent with us. Needless to say, I spent the night watching it bloom, and it bloomed, just for me.

Some days, for no reason at all, tears would just flow, but other days when I look at the sunset, my heart aches a little bit less, for my boy has never really left me.

Our Jack Russell family

By Alison & Bosko Tadic

Lucy and Larry as per below are their current Jack Russells – Lucy is seven years old and Larry is aged five.

I will never forget the date: March 15th 1997. My husband and I had only been married a few months and had talked of getting a puppy in the near future. However, with both of us working full time it wasn't something we had got around to doing.

Lucy and Larry (left to right) *Larry and Lucy (left to right)*

It was a Saturday and I was working in retail and invited to go out to a birthday party that night. Rushing out in my lunch break to purchase a gift, I saw a little crowd of people oohing and aahing around a middle-aged dad with a basket of gorgeous puppies. I thought to myself, I will stop on the way back and check them out.

As I walked back, I only saw one little puppy left with the most adorable face. The man was reading the paper and there was a sign that said "Free to good home." I spoke to the lovely gentleman and he said it was a Jack Russell cross. I hadn't known the breed, having only ever had little Maltese terriers growing up, but I rushed back to work, rang my husband hysterically and said it was just the cutest thing ever. He knew the breed and agreed straight away. I brought him home and it was true love at first sight. We named him Woody and he was so smart, loyal and cherished by both of us. Truly the light of our life.

Two years later, we decided to get him a playmate named Dotty and they were inseparable. She was so sassy and fearless. They went on to have a litter that was born in our very hands, and our world completely revolved around our amazing little fur family.

We kept a boy and girl and gave the rest to family so we could always see them. For the next fourteen years, our life was only about our dogs, and we wouldn't have it any other way. They comforted us through a number of miscarriages, the death of my father, business closure, near bankruptcy and illness.

We hadn't even gone on a holiday, not even a weekend away in over twelve years, so as to not leave them. When Woody first started slowing down and becoming unwell in 2010, the stress was unbelievable. To see your precious fur babies feeling unwell, although we did as much as we absolutely possibly could, was agony. We had no choice but to put him to sleep on August 15th 2012.

We felt our world had ended. We'd had him for over a third of our lives, and the bond was unbreakable. He was buried in our yard under a beautiful umbrella tree next to a peaceful pond that we would visit every day. The impact it had on Dotty, Jacky his daughter and Elwood his son, was deeply felt too.

Over the next few years, with age and illness, we had to say goodbye to them too, and it never got easier. It's a pain I wouldn't wish on my worst enemy. It was really amazing to see friends and family being supportive and understanding too. To some people it's just a dog, but to others they are soulmates.

Going through the motions of everyday life and carrying on with my job was so difficult. You feel like a part of your heart has been ripped out, and not having work colleagues and superiors understand was very difficult. As I have gotten older, I truly feel a deeper connection with friends who feel the same way about their dogs too. Not only are our dogs the best company and heart healers, but they have brought us closer to people and have helped us meet the most amazing friends.

We have now been blessed with another pair of crazy Jack Russells named Lucy and Larry that we love beyond words. They haven't replaced Woody, Dotty, Jacky and Elwood. Instead, we truly believe they sent us Lucy and Larry to heal our pain.

We happened to get Lucy on January 30th which, coincidentally, was Woody's birthday, and through an uncanny series of events that can only be described as signs from above, this crazy little bundle of energy brought life and love back to our home and helped heal our hearts. Larry followed a couple of years later and they are inseparable.

I can't understand how some people say, "They are just a dog." I see the most amazing souls, with gentle personalities that make us laugh every day, give unconditional love and show no judgment whatsoever. Every animal I am blessed to see fills my heart with so much love and joy. There just isn't enough time with our beautiful fur children. ❤

Sparky

By Deb

I never knew I could love an animal with all my heart until a little rescue Jack Russell named Sparky came into my life and joined my family. He was the very best thing to ever happen to my family. He had a heart of gold and loyalty greater than any person I have ever known. He dedicated his life to me and my children, and for that, I am forever grateful. Sparky had a way of giving his time to each member of my family at a level we each needed, and endearing himself to each of us with a love that will last forever.

I discovered Sparky on Christmas Eve. I had been searching for a rescue dog for a long time, and each time I found a terrier available, I would find out it was already adopted, and had accepted that the time wasn't right. When I called the shelter and discovered he was still available, I asked them to hold him for me, and we went immediately to meet him. I will always remember seeing him for the first time, sitting on the bed in the dog enclosure, and then spending time with him in an exercise yard, where he ignored us and ran around barking at other dogs along the fence line and peeing on everything, two characteristics that never changed!

As we sat there, the attendant explained he was surrendered two weeks before Christmas, and no one had called until now, but there was another couple interested in him if we weren't. I asked what they did, and she explained the woman was a dog groomer who worked from home. I instantly thought this person was probably better for Sparky, as we were at work and school, and he would spend long hours alone each day. So, sadly, we walked away, deflated and sad, but knowing it was a better option for this active little boy.

Within half an hour of leaving, I received a call from the shelter and was asked if I was still interested in Sparky. The other people had two cats, and when they "cat tested" Sparky, he showed a lot of interest – another characteristic of Sparky that held true throughout his life!

Immediately, I said yes and paid all the fees over the phone so he could be mine. I was never going to let him go, ever again.

Sparky quickly settled into our home, and we discovered he loved having the house to himself during the day. He would sit in the middle of the couch, or lie on our beds if we left the door open. At that stage, I had two teenagers who always shut their doors, but Sparky soon changed that by dragging his bed into the doorway of my son's room, and would spend each night guarding him, growling if anyone dared to come near the door! This had another effect upon my son – it required him to clean up his room, as Sparky would snuffle through his things, and disrupt his order!

Soon, Sparky managed to work his way onto my bed, and I realised just how comforting it is to sleep next to a dog. He soon worked his way into my daughter's room to win her over too, having cuddles and spending time together, going for walks or just hanging out. There are so many Sparky stories, but the greatest gift was the little dog who would stay by our sides through the hardships of life, the teenage years, but also the major upheavals I experienced as an adult – without Sparky, they would have ended so very differently.

People talk about the ups and downs of life, but sometimes those downs are very, very low. I was the victim of severe workplace bullying over several years, which led to a breakdown, and me leaving work to recover. Sparky was my constant companion and the calming influence that gave me peace and reassurance each day as I healed. I think the fact dogs don't talk is their greatest gift, as all their expression is nonverbal. It is comfort and compassion, not expectation, and they never give unwanted advice, just validation that we are loved, needed and important.

It was during this recovery that I became the lead witness in a serious criminal investigation and trial, and went into hiding until the person went to prison, where they are still sitting, right where they belong. However, I find myself once again fighting to keep this person behind bars as they apply for parole.

The trial took several years and was mentally and emotionally exhausting, and I withdrew into a seriously severe depression, sleeping eighteen hours a day, barely able to function, to the point where I decided to take my own life. With that decision, I felt a flood of relief, knowing the pain would be over. However, beside me lay Sparky. My children were grown and I'd convinced myself they would be better off without me, but here was my elderly boy, always by my side, faithful and loving, but as dependent upon me as I was upon him. So, because of this little dog named Sparky, I didn't end my life, and I am here now to talk about just how wonderful he was.

For those who say, "It's just a dog," they have missed out on knowing great love, and loyalty so deep, that years after that little dog dies, you can sob at the memory of that loss. It is "the tear that hangs inside my soul for ever." I write this through tears of joy and pain for my soulmate, my sweet boy, Sparky xxoo.

Liberty

By Brooke Delaney

I had not long lost my beloved Weimaraner Jazz from a GDV, when a beautiful tri-coloured Cavalier King Charles Spaniel came into my life. Known as Lady, she was stunning to look at, but way too boisterous for her old home. How could one little Cavalier cause so many problems for her owners? An opportunity arose for her to find a loving home, which I took, and I never looked back.

She was cheeky, but loved by children, and when she looked at you, it was enough to steal your heart. I knew that to keep her I would need to change her name and start afresh to help modify the learned behaviour traits that caused her to be rehomed. She was an elegant-looking dog with a mind of her own, so the name in the end was easy: “Liberty” after the Statue of Liberty. It means freedom. We would call her “Libby” for short.

As she adjusted to her new family – me, my six-year-old daughter Myiah and our cat Mishka – it was clear she needed some basic training with distractions, as she was very easily distracted. We enrolled her in the local obedience school where she repeated the beginner’s stage twice. It was here that her love of children and other animals and people became apparent, and from then on she was my work dog.

We started by visiting the local high school for careers day. I had previously attended with my Weimaraner Jazz, so I knew what to expect. At Libby’s first visit, the teachers were shocked at the passing of Jazz but also very happy to meet Libby. In true Libby fashion, she stole everyone’s heart by walking towards the teachers wagging her tail and enjoying pats and looking into everyone’s eyes. Her next step was on stage in front of many teachers, business representatives and year ten students. She encouraged many to go on to ask further questions, and even attend work experience at local vet surgeries in the area.

I couldn’t be prouder of the way little Libby behaved and the emotional connections she made in such a short amount of time. Libby soon became my sidekick, and we attended many preschools and primary schools to help educate children and teachers how to pat a dog safely. During our adventures, there were many moments where little Libby touched children's hearts. Two came to mind vividly and each moment made me love her more and more.

At one particular school in a country town, there were many children who had farm dogs, and one particular child had been bitten badly on the face at the age of four and was now terrified of dogs. The child sat at the back of the room on their teacher's lap the entire presentation and watched from a distance. This talk was very much needed at this particular school based on some of the responses of the children.

During the delta dog presentation, the main result is to teach children when it is safe to pat a happy dog, and things to avoid depending on body language when they see a dog acting in a particular way. There are three main rules: 1) Ask the adult in charge of them on a particular day if it's okay to pat the happy dog (teacher at school or preschool) 2) Ask the owner of the dog (the dog may not like children or may be sick or injured) 3) Walk gently towards the happy dog showing them a gentle fist to sniff, and if they don't react, pat them down the side of the chest.

In our situation, the children could pat the stuffed dog or the live dog. After seeing how gentle Libby was, the little one at the back who had been scared, asked the teacher if he could pat the dog. The teacher held his hand whilst he approached, and he asked me if it was okay to pat the dog, and he then asked the dog ever so gently. Little Libby looked into his eyes and wagged her tail. He gently patted Libby and stayed patting her for what seemed like hours whilst teachers took photos and his whole class told him how proud they were. Dogs may not be able to talk but they can definitely communicate with body language.

Another time, in a disability class, a little hearing-impaired child asked his teacher through sign language if it was okay. Little Libby stood at his wheelchair on two hindlimbs when he put his hand down, and then she gently licked him on his hand and his ear. When he bent down to pat the side of her chest, she looked lovingly into his eyes – such behaviours can't be trained into a dog. Libby knew when to work and when to just be a dog.

She helped raise many litters of kittens, and helped many of the junior nurses with their grooming assignments. She always behaved on cue and enjoyed a good clip and bath. At home, she was a normal four-legged family member. She adjusted well to our ever-growing blended family with more humans – a dad and two more kids to play with – and many four-legged friends that would become new besties. Libby enjoyed bush walks, swims at Yarramundi and escaping episodes, including under the neighbour's fence in the rain and through the doggy door covered in mud to wake her up by jumping on her white bed sheets and kissing her. She was always returned well-loved.

Over the years, Libby had many vet adventures as well – eye ulcers, walking into things, ear infections, dentals, and in her older years when her new friend Emba kindly rounded up a snake, little Libby thought she would get close enough to its head to be bitten, and received antivenom. After this little adventure, Libby developed a heart murmur and was started on cardiac medications and regularly saw her medical specialist and cardiologist.

Libby took us by surprise late last year on November 8th. Hubby found her dazed first thing in the morning and unable to get up. At first he thought it was her heart and gave her the morning heart medication prior to calling to bring her in, as she'd been her normal self the night before. He dropped little Ash to school and brought Libby and her sister Emba down to the vet's. On arrival, she was drooling and very vacant-looking. The team worked on her together as I was very upset. I continued to see other patients for the day, while the rest of the team worked on Libby. She was in a critical state and was referred to the specialist hospital.

I immediately began crying, as I knew her doctor was on leave that week. She really needed a holiday, as she is the most dedicated vet I have met in my twenty-two year career. You get so attached to your pet's vet that sometimes, in emergency situations, all common sense goes out the window as you just focus on getting your pet well. I bundled Libby and Emba in the car for the journey to the specialist's and rang her specialist, crying. She organised for the critical care specialist to see Libby on her behalf, and my husband left work to meet us all there. On arrival, I called reception and they sent a triage nurse out to collect Libby and take her to the critical care specialists. We waited with Emba in the dog run outside (Covid times) for what seemed like an eternity.

After about an hour, the specialist came out to speak with us. Libby was anaemic on presentation; her blood count had dropped to fifteen per cent. The cause for her anaemia was thought to be immune mediated haemolytic anaemia (IMHA). This is a condition where the immune system attacks and destroys the red blood cells. I was familiar with this disease and knew she had a fight ahead of her. She had further tests to see if she had an underlying condition that had triggered this disease. Nothing was found. We decided to go ahead with therapy for IMHA and hope that she would respond. It usually takes about four to five days to see a response, and during this time she would need to be supported with intravenous fluids and immunosuppressive therapy.

She was connected to a lot of fluid pumps and monitors. When her specialist called the next day, Libby was stable but still had a long way to go. I visited her every afternoon, as I did not want her to think we had forgotten about her. When we visited, because of Covid restrictions, we had to put on PPE and see her in a special room. She looked so sick and often was too weak to respond to me as she normally would.

One afternoon, I was considering whether to continue with therapy, and my dear friend called on FaceTime. Lynn had been Libby's previous vet for many years, and although Libby did not lift her head for me that night, she knew exactly who Lynn was. She lifted her head and moved towards my phone. To me, that was a sign that she hadn't given up. It reminded me of a song by Jason Mraz, *I won't give up*. How could I give up on her when she had given my family and children in the community so much love? I just couldn't do it.

Libby was fighting the fight of her life when Bear also became very unwell. Jody and I met through Bear, and talking to Jody, I knew we shared such common values and a dear love for our best friends, Libby and Bear. I so wanted to be there for Jody when she was saying goodbye to Bear and when Bear gained her angel wings, but I was with my girl Libby asking her to hold on and fight. We took each day at a time, visiting daily, praying and hoping. On the Saturday that week, her vet called me and said Libby needed an urgent sodium bicarbonate infusion, as she was the sickest patient in the hospital.

At this stage, I was working my second job and had to take some time off. My boss at the café is one of the loveliest people you could ever meet and knew how much little Libby meant to me. Throughout Libby's hospital stay, she checked on me every day to make sure I was okay and asked how Libby was doing. I was upset during the rest of my shift, and of course, when the new Adele song, *Easy On Me,* came on the radio, I tried my best to not cry, but I could only ever think of Lib during this song. I visited her after work that night due to how critical she was and was glad I did. It was crazy there. It was after ten p.m. and I appreciated them organising a visit. They were literally running around, trying to look after multiple patients at the time.

It's amazing the people you meet while waiting to visit your pet, people who don't understand the pressure the vet industry is under at present. They would complain to me about the wait time of getting their well patients back, and I would always respond saying they were pretty busy dealing with multiple sick patients. Once, I visited and waited extra-long as a patient had had a cardiac arrest. They rang my mobile to inform me, and at the time I was thankful it was not Libby, but also did feel sorrow for the family whose patient had arrested. I explained to many that it's okay to wait a while if you get to take your pet home. I was really just hoping I got to take my girl home. This often changed people's views, and they had calmed down by the time their pet was discharged. Instead of them being upset with the vet, they were often thankful.

After almost a week, I had a routine. While driving to work, I would call reception for a morning update and see if Libby had made it through the night. She was still fighting but getting weaker. Her specialist returned and said she was concerned about kidney function, as her urine production was reducing and her kidney enzymes were very high. She had acute kidney injury and it was thought this was secondary to the pigment from her destroyed red blood cells damaging her kidneys. If her urine production didn't improve, her chances of recovery were not good.

We were all so worried about Lib. The next few days were very hard. Ash, Emba and I visited her again the next day, and she appeared weaker. Emba must have sensed how unwell she was and immediately went to her and started licking her face. It was an impossible decision to make. Should we stop therapy and let her go? Her specialist let us spend some time with Libby, as she knew it was a difficult decision to make. If she didn't start producing a larger amount of urine soon, then her chances of recovery were poor.

Just at that moment, she did produce a little urine. It wasn't much but it was something. I decided to give her another twenty-four hours. Ash, Emba and I made the long journey home and a few tears were shed. I knew it wasn't looking good and I prayed for a miracle.

That night I slept with Emba on the couch, as she was sad and missing her friend. My mobile rang at one a.m. It was the overnight vet calling to let me know he thought Libby was deteriorating and wanted to give me the option of coming to say goodbye, as he was not sure she was going to survive the night.

Emba and I made the journey down to say goodbye. When we arrived, we were put into a room with Libby. Emba was concerned and kept walking around sniffing, then going to the corner of the room. After we said goodbye, I let the vet know it was okay – it was time. He very slowly and gently gave Libby the medicine to put her to sleep. She went so peacefully, and Emba immediately walked to the corner of the room and stayed there, keeping her distance but also watching over her. It was a very long and sad drive back to the mountains. It was like there was a huge whole in my heart. I spent the day with Emba, who did not want to leave my side. It was hard.

I didn't feel like eating or sleeping, just crying. I did not feel like being around other clients' pets, especially Cavalier King Charles Spaniels, so I took a few days off. My first day back was hard. The first admission of the day was for a dental, and when I went to the car for Covid consulting to go through the forms and bring in the patient, I realised it was a ruby Cavalier. I had to hold back the tears. It was so hard. I got through it and made friends with our adorable patient. The first nurse consult of the day was a blood check on a recovering patient who made it through IMHA. A beautiful patient and client, but she made it through. Why couldn't my Libby?

Life is hard sometimes, very hard. Later that week, I brought Libby's ashes home. I sat in the kitchen for hours and hours and hours just holding her, crying, asking myself what I could have done differently that may have helped save her. It was at this time my husband thought maybe another dog might help. I didn't know what I thought about that at first, but after some checking on Google, I found a Weimaraner breeder in the blue mountains. I could never get another Cavalier, at least not yet, but I possibly could consider another Weimaraner. I left a message with the breeder, and the next day she called me and asked where I'd found her details. She said it just so happened someone using her bloodline had a litter of puppies, and she asked if she could give them my number.

Before long, I received a call from the breeder who was trained in the delta dog ways and had a country property where the puppies would grow up with horses and cows, and the mother's name was Faith. I think this was a sign. We decided to get the family a puppy for Christmas, and although she wasn't ready for a few weeks, we felt that this is what Libby would have wanted for Emba and for the family, and to continue her work as the delta dog to help teach kids dog safety. Before long, it was time to pick our baby up. Ash and I made the long journey to the country, where we met our little girl who we'd bring home and later call Iluka (by the Sea), ILY for short (I Love You). As we turned the corner to pick up our girl, we noticed the business on the corner was called LIBERTY. I think it was meant to be, as this was Libby's way of saying it's okay to move on.

On our long journey back, we saw a bunch of clouds in the sky shaped like a dog's head and angel wings. In my heart, as I drove and looked out the window, I thought, "I will always love you Lib, but

I know you want me to move on and I know you would love this boisterous, sprightly, courageous, stunning-looking girl." Iluka hated the crate at first, just like Libby, and she also liked to eat everything in sight, just like Libby. At the end of our first week with Iluka, her dogs papers came through: "Tyrilbee Field Of Dreams."

Thank you little Libby – your spirit and your training will live on. We will continue to speak of you and your presence in this world, and the love you gave us.

Conclusion

Pets have the ability to save people's lives. They are truly inspirational. Let's face it, pets are therapeutic and can be the best medication. We have guide dogs that provide sight for the visually impaired, and we have assistance dogs who assist a variety of people. We also have therapy pets that visit sick kids in hospital and nursing homes to brighten the elderly's days.

We also have police dogs who are trained to track down criminals. Horses are used to assist people with PTSD – there have been many studies done on this. They always manage to bring love and a smile to anyone's face, no matter the challenge. They say laughter is the best medicine but I believe our pets are the best medicine. Pets really can do amazing things with the right person by their side, and love and compassion.

This book also highlights the amazing work our vet practices do. After all, they are the unsung heroes. They look after, treat and care for our pets and save our pets' lives. They also form bonds with pet and owner. They are the forgotten ones in this journey, and they also grieve the loss of our pets with us as we do.

I feel employers and workplaces need more awareness about the challenge a person faces when grieving the loss of a pet. After all, they are a big part of our family. People feel that when they lose a pet and are grieving, they can't tell their workplace in case of lack of support or acknowledgement for that pet, and I would love to see changes made in this space.

I wrote the book I hoped to find and read. I wanted to read a person's personal story. I hope this book helps anyone who is currently grieving the loss of a pet and provides a level of comfort along with validation that your thoughts and feelings are very real. This journey of grief is debilitating – it is okay not to be okay, but if you are struggling, please reach out. There are people, such as bereavement counsellors, who specialise in grief relating to the loss of a pet, along with Facebook groups that offer much support. I have been a part of such Facebook groups.

My hope is that workplace policies will change and be inclusive of pets and pet parents, and see pet parents as another diverse group. Employers need to see there is a real need to be inclusive of all groups and that the pandemic has changed the pet industry. More families have taken on pets, whereas before the pandemic they worked full time and didn't have the time to introduce a pet or take care of a pet. Most families have a pet, and in some cases, multiple pets like myself.

Our vet industry is struggling with suicide and depression and many are under-resourced. While the vet industry boomed when the pandemic hit, the vet industry also struggled. Vets and vet nurses walked away from their profession due to stress and pressure from numerous sources, lack of empathy from pet parents abusing them for the costs of treatments and wait times and the emotional impact of performing numerous euthanasias, along with more pets requiring vet treatment.

Our vet teams are pretty amazing people. They are full of love and compassion, not just for pets but for us as pet owners. With these types of people walking away from their profession, it is going to cause longer wait times for pets to be seen, and in some cases practices closing their doors as they are unable to fill vacancies. This is already being seen from the only practice in Parkes (regional NSW) closing its door due to staffing constraints, and more recently a practice very close to me at Mulgoa.

This book is for my precious Bear. It is her legacy, but it is for everyone. Everyone's journey is individual and special and all our pets are equally special. They bring so much love and joy to our lives and it is unequivocally unconditional – it is pure and genuine. For all of you who have read this book, I am sending my love and thoughts, and my heart aches for the grief you are experiencing.

RIP to all our fur babies who have touched our lives and grown their angel wings.

Resources

Pet Bereavement Counsellors (most pet bereavement counsellors have been through their own personal loss of a pet) – state-wide.

Vicky Nonas – By My Side Pet Bereavement Counsellor in Sydney Australia
(proud sponsor of The Bear Project)
www.bymyside.net.au

Sharlene Crofts – Pet Bereavement Counsellor in Sydney Australia (proud sponsor of The Bear Project)
sharlenescounsellingservices@yahoo.com

Kelly's Animal Communications
(proud sponsor of The Bear Project)
www.kellysanimalcommunication.com.au

Comfort Cuddles – Kaylene Dore
www.comfortcuddles.com.au
https://www.facebook.com/comfortcuddlesaustralia

Lifeline Australia 13 11 14
Lifeline Australia - 13 11 14 - Crisis Support. Suicide Prevention.

1800RESEPECT (1800 737 732) – National domestic, family and sexual violence counselling
Home | 1800RESPECT

Various Facebook pet loss support groups within Australia and all over the world. I have joined a couple of these and found them comforting, as there are so many like-minded people.

Sponsors of the Bear Project

A very big thank you to my sponsors, as this book could not have been published without you.

I couldn't have done this without my sponsors, who are listed below:

Physioinq South Penrith / Penrith
Owner & Principal Physiotherapist: Christopher Slaviero
https://www.southpenrithphysio.com.au

I have been a patient with Chris and his team for various injuries over the past six years and highly recommend them. They are not only extremely professional, but caring, kind and understanding of your injury. Their knowledge is extensive and second to none. They work with you through your rehabilitation journey. As a patient, you couldn't be in any better hands.

Chris was the very first sponsor to join this journey, fully supporting grieving pet parents.

It would be hard to find a better physiotherapist this side of Sydney. Thank you, Chris for joining The Bear Project.

Kelly's Animal Communication
Owner: Kelly Mercieca
www.kellysanimalcommunication.com.au

I first met Kelly around a year and a half ago when I had a reading with her for my two pets, Sunny the horse and Bear who has now since passed. Bear was still alive at the time I had my reading with Kelly. Kelly told me about Bear's arthritis, along with the guilt I was carrying when I had to part with Sunny. Sunny and I have since been reunited. Kelly provided me with kindness and compassion, but above all, answers which provided a great deal of comfort. I would highly recommend Kelly for a reading. She was also one of the first to come on board as a sponsor with the book in full support of my aim to comfort grieving pet parents. Thank you, Kelly, for joining The Bear Project.

JB Fabweld
Jason Bradshaw
jbbfabweld@gmail.com

I have known Jason personally and professionally for twenty-two years. During this time, Jason completed work at my parents home (pergola) and also friends' homes. Jason is a metal fabricator, whose work ranges from sheet metal to structural steel. Jason's workshop is a factory at St Marys, or he can complete jobs on site depending on the size of the job, as he is a sole trader. Work specialities are framework, truck and trailer refurbishing, handrailing, balustrades, welding (tig and mig) with the use of mild steel, stainless steel and aluminium. Jason is a perfectionist. Every job is completed with one hundred percent satisfaction, and there is no job too big or too small. Thank you, Jason, for joining The Bear Project.

Pet Bereavement Counsellor
Sharlene Crofts
sharlenescounsellingservices@yahoo.com

I met Sharlene through the Jack Russells Down Under Facebook group, which we both have been a part of for a few years. Sharlene was one of the first people on the group to reach out to me privately to check in and let me know she was there for support. At the time, I didn't know Sharlene was a pet bereavement counsellor. She gave me her contact details. Over the months, I have grown to know Sharlene personally and professionally. You will find it hard to find a nicer, more understanding, kind-hearted soul. Sharlene has been on her own journey as a pet parent, experiencing grief first-hand when she lost her beautiful fur baby Diesel. She knows the journey not only as a counsellor but a pet parent. If you require counselling, please reach out to Sharlene. Anyone who mentions this book will receive 10% off counselling services. Thank you, Sharlene for joining The Bear Project.

Bovercon Pty Ltd
Director: Edward Breedveld
www.bovercon.com.au

Bovercon specializes and prides themselves in compliances and certifications for council fire orders, construction and building management. Strong project leadership parallel to on-time concept completions. They are highly client-focused with first rate quality and service, coupled with competitive pricing, always. Thank you Ed, for joining The Bear Project.

Comfort Cuddles
Kaylene Dore
www.comfortcuddles.com.au

Comfort Cuddles has designed a plush soft toy dog and cat to help people to cope with the loss of a much-loved pet who has crossed the Rainbow Bridge. Comfort Cuddles companions have wings and a discrete pouch in their tummy to hold a pet's ID tag, collar or lock of fur. When our pets leave us, we often wish we could have had one last cuddle. Having a memento of your pet in a Comfort Cuddles companion, which you can hold close and cuddle, can bring healing, especially to children and long-time pet owners who would just love to have "one last cuddle."

Comfort Cuddles companions aren't meant to be a replica of your pet. Your pet was unique. Having a more generic dog or cat can remind us of our much-loved pet while allowing us to move along our grieving journey. Thank you, Kaylene, for joining The Bear Project.

Assistance Dogs in Training Australia
Kaylene Dore
https://www.adita.com.au/

Assistance Dogs in Training Australia (ADiTA) provides information and support to people embarking on the journey of purchasing or training an Assistance Dog. Millions of Australians enjoy the companionship of pets in their home. Assistance Dogs, and Assistance Dogs in Training, provide much more than companionship. ADs and ADiTs are trained to specifically provide assistance to a person with a disability, including people with vision loss, hearing loss, mobility issues, Autism, PTSD and other invisible disabilities. Knowing their Assistance Dog is specifically trained to support them can increase a person's independence and social participation.

ADiTA is committed to providing information and support to people with a disability and their Assistance Dog or Assistance Dog in Training, as well as providing information and education to the wider community on how they too can support people with an Assistance Dog or Assistance Dog in Training. Thank you Kaylene, for joining The Bear Project.

Rotary Club of Wallacia
Mulgoa Valley

The benefits of being a Rotarian are many and varied. Being part of an organisation that is international allows you to connect with Rotarians internationally, nationally and in your local community. Perhaps what most Rotarians say is being a Rotarian allows you to help others "to build a better world," to take action and make a difference, form friendships with like-minded people, and have fun. Thank you, Rotary Club, for joining The Bear Project.

Penrith Veterinary Hospital
www.penrithvet.com.au

For over fifty years, Penrith Veterinary Hospital has been helping pets, rural and wild animals. What started as a single veterinarian practice, Penrith Vets has grown to include seven fully certified veterinarians and a dedicated, caring and experienced nursing and reception staff. Our owners, Mathew and Sally, are a married couple who work at the hospital. They are passionate about helping animals live happy and healthy lives, and providing gentle and compassionate care when pets are unwell. Whatever your pet's needs, you will find modern treatments and friendly advice at Penrith Vets. Thank you, Matthew for joining The Bear Project.

Kristine's K9 Treats
https://www.kristinesk9kakesandtreats.com.au

At Kristine's K9 Kakes and Treats, we pride ourselves on delivering the best, 100% natural, human grade, no added nasties, treats for your four-legged pals. We are proud to be Australian-made and owned, and only source the best local ingredients to ensure the treats you are buying are the quality you deserve. We believe our four-legged pals deserve the same love and treatment we give humans, and that is why we put so much love and time in to making the perfect treats for them. Thank you Kristine for joining The Bear Project.

Pet Bereavement Counsellor
Vicky Nonas
www.bymyside.net.au
www.facebook.com/Bymysideau
Facebook Private Support Group:
https://www.facebook.com/groups/107795198224685

"With great love comes great loss."

If you have ever had a beloved pet that has owned your heart, you would know that losing them can be extremely painful.

Vicky Nonas is well acquainted with grief. From her lived experience, including the loss of her beloved Cattle x Kelpie, Boof in 2009. she felt what can only be described as a strong pull to one day support others in their time of need - something she says, "that was sadly lacking when she needed help with her heartbreak."

As a Specialist Pet Bereavement and Grief Counsellor, Vicky can be found most of her time offering a safe space for clients in which they can express their sorrow and talk about the fond forever memories of their beloved pets. She offers a deep witnessing and acknowledgement of this underestimated grief, and a knowing that, for many, losing a beloved pet can be just as significant as losing a human loved one, perhaps more so for some people.

If you would like to know more about Vicky and what she is doing, head over to By My Side - Pet Loss Counselling. Thank you, Vicky for joining The Bear Project.

Selwood House Veterinary Hospital is set in the beautiful grounds of a heritage listed house in Hazelbrook.

We are a local family-owned clinic and have an experienced team of seven vets and over ten passionate nurses dedicated to the pets of the Blue Mountains. With over one hundred and twenty years of combined experience, our vets' interests and further education range from behaviour, avian medicine, pathology, dentistry, surgery & feline medicine.

Our aim is compassionate care, with up-to-date knowledge, equipment and treatments, helping you to find the right solution for your pets' problems.

When the time comes to say goodbye, we have a private, peaceful area of the heritage garden, or if the weather is not appropriate, we have a separate private room away from the rest of the clinic that can be used if needed. Thank you Lawrence for joining The Bear Project.

Acknowledgements

Very big special thanks to the below people who supported, loved and nurtured me through my great loss of Bear. I couldn't have gone through this without you.

- My mum
- Dina Franks (this book wouldn't have been written without you)
- Crysten Hall (Vet nurse from my local vet)
- Brooke Delaney (Vet nurse from my local vet)
- Michelle Okorn (Vet from my local vet) All the vets, vet nurses and reception staff (from my local vet) – such an amazing bunch of people – you all touched Bear's life as well as my own
- Alison and Bosko Tadic – have been there for me every single step and breath I took
- Mark and Julie Kendrigan
- Jacinta Carter

There are so many other people to thank. In the meantime, thank you to each and every one who checked in, sent messages, flowers and cards, made sure I was eating but gave me a shoulder to cry on and an ear to listen to. The support I was shown during this time was beautiful and something I will never forget, even from complete strangers who could see my distress and asked if I was okay. I found so many compassionate people who do care.

Very big thank you to those of you have contributed to my GoFundMe. Without you, along with my sponsors, this book wouldn't be published.

I would also like to say a very special and big thank you to Cherelle Trevethan, who kindly produced my logo. I highly recommend Cherelle for any design logos. When we spoke, Cherelle took the time to learn about my vision for my logo and what I wanted my logo to look like. She asked questions and made suggestions. Cherelle developed the perfect logo with an uncanny representation of Bear (replicated from a photo).

When I saw the logo, I was ecstatic. It was perfect, exactly what I wanted. I actually cried to think that Cherelle could see my vision from our talk. Thank you, Cherelle, I don't think anyone else would have done this logo justice.

Cherelle is a Graphic Designer and Illustrator, details as follows:
Cherelle Trevethan
0425 754 368
cherelletrevethan.myportfolio.com

About the Author

I grew up in the Western Suburbs of Sydney and have lived here most of my life. Twelve years ago, I lived in a remote location in a small country town called Goodooga for three and a half years. This taught me a lot about myself and gave me a new appreciation for not living near a big city. I guess you could say my dream now is to own acreage and have lots of pets – I now love country life.

I work as a personal assistant for a government department. Over the years, I have completed a Small Business Management Course CERT IV acquiring credits, along with a Business Diploma acquiring distinctions. I am currently also completing an Executive Assistant course which will accompany accreditation.

I have always had a passion and love for all animals. When I was young, I wanted to be a vet, but that dream didn't come to fruition. The pets I currently have are a dog (Angel), a horse (Sunny), a cat (Puss) and a rabbit (Nala). One of my passions is horse riding. I am currently taking lessons and I love going on trail rides. I really enjoy going to the gym and training with like-minded people. This is my first book. I never thought I would do something like this, let alone believed it would happen. It just goes to show we are capable of anything if we put our heart and soul into it, and more importantly, if we believe in ourselves.

www.ingramcontent.com/pod-product-compliance
Ingram Content Group UK Ltd.
Pitfield, Milton Keynes, MK11 3LW, UK
UKHW062302290726
14090UKWH00017B/850

9 780645 621303